THE LITTLE
BLACK BOOK OF
BRAIN GAMES

Suzanne Beilenson

D0211851

WHITE PLAINS, NEW YORK

*For Tommy...whose sharp wits are
quickly making him a puzzle master!*

Designed by Margaret Rubiano

Illustrations by David Cole Wheeler
and Margaret Rubiano

Copyright © 2009
Peter Pauper Press, Inc.
202 Mamaroneck Ave.
White Plains, NY 10601
ISBN 978-1-59359-768-9
Printed in China
7 6 5 4 3 2 1

Visit us at www.peterpauper.com

THE LITTLE
BLACK BOOK OF
BRAIN GAMES

Contents

Introduction

Question: What measures
6" x 3-1/2" and provides hours
of entertainment, yet makes
time stand still?

Answer: *The Little Black Book
of Brain Games,* of course!

We've packed this book chock-full of puzzles,
posers, and problems that will so engross you,
you'll lose all track of time. But don't worry.
You won't lose anything else. In fact, the more
you play, the more you'll gain.

Research shows that play "lights up" the
brain. While you're cogitating on each of our
absorbing brainteasers, you will be building
your cognitive powers. You will sharpen your
reasoning skills, improve your memory,
enhance your creativity, and foster your mental flexibility.

Puzzles and play are not just for kids. Adults need mental engagement just as much, if not more so—it's not as if we still sit in a classroom every day stretching our brains to understand osmosis or how to parse a poem. We need to find other ways to stimulate ourselves and our brains. You've found an entertaining way with *The Little Black Book of Brain Games*. It's your handy companion on the road to mental strength.

What's more, as you try to solve each puzzle, it's not just your brain reaping the benefits. You will relieve stress and reach that near meditative state of "flow" where the outside world seems to drop away. Less stress and more flow in your life add up to greater happiness. Now, there's one great piece of arithmetic!

So, get started now. In each chapter of *The Little Black Book of Brain Games,* you'll find a different type of brain game, ranging from tricky math problems and logic games to riddles and word scrambles. Some are easy and some are downright cunning, but all call upon your mental acuity.

If at first you don't succeed, well—try, try again. Don't be too quick to flip to the answers in the back of the book. Success can be yours if you persevere, and you will be surprised at how a solution may come to you if you return to the same puzzle later. Some solutions involve strategies of pattern recognition or critical reasoning, while others require you to forgo logic, and think outside the box altogether.

Remember, different types of puzzles exercise different parts of your brain. If one game type proves more baffling than another, you definitely want to spend some extra time toying with those puzzles because that's how you'll strengthen your overall mental capacity.

Give yourself a brain boost and get those synapses firing. Our collection of entertaining and intriguing mind-benders awaits your pleasure.

WELCOME TO THE WACKY WORLD OF WORD GAMES. For all you wily wordsmiths out there, these brain ticklers are just for you! Letters are scrambled and words have gone missing. To succeed, you will need to play with letters, look for patterns, and scour your working vocabulary. Above all, you'll need to engage your sense of play—because these word games are designed to entertain and enlighten. But if a puzzle type seems familiar, take a second look. We've put a new spin on some old favorites. Also, be advised: the puzzles get more challenging as you proceed.

So use all of the talents and tools at your brain's disposal, but whatever you do, do not peek in the dictionary. After all, that just wouldn't be any fun!

1 The Glue Word!

A Glue Word is one that makes sense with both the first word and the last word given. For example, the Glue Word for PLAY _____ BEEF is "Ground."

A. MISTLE _____ HOLD

B. EGG _____ CALL

C. MARKET _____ MAT

D. HIGH _____ BEAT

E. LONG _____ RIOT

F. TWIN _____ HEAD

G. COUNTER _____ QUOTIENT

* * *

2 A Simple Scramble

Arrange the following letters so that they will spell just one word:

ENOTSUJDROW

_____

3 Missing States

If you add the same letter a certain number of times, you will get the name of a State. It may or may not be the same letter for each State:

VRGNA

MIIIPPI

TNNSS

LBM

LLNOS

HI

CLRAD

REGN

LSK

④ Opposites Attract

Below are 9 pairs of opposites. The only thing these attractive antonyms are missing is the first letter of each word. Can you fill in the correct letters?

A. ___ORMAL   ___ELAXED

B. ___IVELY   ___ULL

C. ___RONE   ___RECT

D. ___OMMON   ___CARCE

E. ___IDE   ___ARROW

F. ___UDDING   ___ITHERED

G. ___CE   ___OVICE

H. ___EIGHTY   ___HALLOW

I. ___REST   ___OTTOM

5 A Proverbial Poser

Unscramble the letters in each group and then rearrange the words to form a well-known adage:

TYSADE CEAR NAD HET NWIS WOSL

_____

_____

_____

* * *

6 A 5-Star Word

Can you think of a common five-letter word that contains, besides itself, five other common words without rearranging the order of the letters or skipping any letters of the original word? For example, "LEASH" contains "ASH" but "LASH" doesn't count as it skips over the "E".

Each word below can be shortened to form a new word by deleting one letter at a time, but not changing the order of the letters. For example, PAINT can be shortened to PANT to PAN to AN to A. How far can you get with SPLASH?

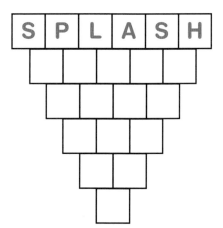

8 A Puzzle of a President

These four words, scrambled together, will spell the name of one of the Presidents of the United States. Do you know who it is?

ROOSTER DOVE THE LEO

_____

* * *

9 Switcheroo!

The words below have nothing in common—until you switch one letter in each word. The new words will have a common theme!

GRANGE   _____

TREAD   _____

THICK   _____

BUMPKIN   _____

MARK   _____

WATCH   _____

Hit the open road and see the country. Along the way, you see these tricky license plates. Can you decipher them?

XLR8	D 2R
GT E UP	A10TION
EXQZME	SR4GRL
2M8O	FOTOGR4
N10S	LOIMVE
NTHUZST	MIL1ION
007 TRADR	AV8R
H20UW8N4	

11 The Mystery Box

Each clue suggests a seven-letter word beginning with S and ending in R. When you have placed all of your answers in the diagram, the seven-letter word down the middle will reveal the box's mystery!

S						R	An office tool
S						R	A knitted garment
S						R	Thin
S						R	One who serves in the army
S						R	An academic
S						R	Not as tall
S						R	Elected representative

⑫ Doublets: An Introduction

Lewis Carroll, best known as the author of *Alice's Adventures in Wonderland,* invented the game of Doublets. In his words, here is how the puzzle works:

"The rules of the Puzzle are simple enough. Two words are proposed, of the same length, and the Puzzle consists in linking these together by interposing other words, each of which shall differ from the next word in one letter only. That is to say, one letter may be changed in one of the given words, then one letter in the word so obtained, and so on, till we arrive at the other given word. The letters must not be interchanged among themselves, but each must keep to its own place."

For example, here's how to turn SAD into FUN (in 3 steps) and REST into SOFA (in 5 steps):

SAD	REST
FAD	LEST
FAN	LOST
FUN	LOFT
	SOFT
	SOFA

A. CAN YOU TURN A DOG INTO A CAT? (IN 3 STEPS)

DOG

_____

_____

CAT

B. CHANGE TEA INTO HOT (IN 4 STEPS)

TEA

_____

_____

_____

HOT

13 An International Mix-Up

The letters of the following words, when rearranged, spell the names of countries. How many can you unscramble?

WENEDS	SUSIRA
MERYGAN	DOLPAN
TENDWARZILS	COXIME
VOIBLIA	KRANDEM
HANDOLL	CRANEF
LEENUVEZA	CROOCOM
HANIC	

Riddle

Mary's father has five daughters: 1. Nana, 2. Nene, 3. Nini, 4. Nono. What is the name of the fifth daughter?

Answer: Mary. The answer was given at the beginning of the question.

14 CryptoList: Ice Cream Flavors

Two scoops? At a certain ice cream parlor, you see the following list of ice cream flavors. Unfortunately, each letter in the original text has been substituted with another. For example, T becomes A, R becomes K, etc. The same code is used throughout the entire list. Can you break the code and get your sundae?

MRPPWO DWYHX

FPOHIMWOOZ

XWHDVKAPHX

YGVYVKHPW YGAD

NOWXYG SHXAKKH

YVVCAWF HXJ YOWHT

DOHKAXW DWYHX

YGWOOZ

YVNNWW

OVYCZ OVHJ

15 Build-a-Word Starter Set

In the puzzle below, each row contains the same three-letter word, though its position may change from row to row. A clue is given for each row. Can you solve this Build-a-Word?

| Play a role |
| A truth |
| Desert plants |
| Existing in fact |
| Farm vehicle |
| Break, as a rib |
| Moral quality |
| Cave hanging |
| Hard to manage |

Riddle

What is the beginning of eternity,
The end of time and space,
The beginning of every end,
And the end of every race?

Answer: The letter E

16 Box Cross

Here are two puzzles that will keep the synapses firing. Fill in the squares with letters, one letter to a square, so that when you are finished, the squares will read the same from left to right, and from top to bottom. The first words in each have been filled in.

F	L	O	P
L			
O			
P			

M	E	A	N
E			
A			
N			

17 Jumble Gym!

If you're a real wordster, then this jumble gym will be lots of fun! Use the 9 letters in the jumble box below to build the word that answers each clue below. Each word must incorporate the central E. Here's a bonus question for you: What thinker uses all nine of the letters?

5 Letters	6 Letters
Horse	Afraid
Gaze	An alcove
Lock of hair	Confidential
Container	
Swap	

7 Letters
After-dinner treat
Made
Calms

8 Letters
Stroked

* * *

18 Matchmaker, Matchmaker!

For each group of four words below, there is one word that goes with all of them. Can you find the match?

DOOR, SESAME, HOUSE, UP

_____

COLD, WALL, AGE, HEAD

_____

TABLE, OUT, WORN, ZONE

_____

COLOR, RUNNING, CLOSET, FRONT

_____

🅳 Lucky Letters

Here's a puzzle that looks easy, but proves tricky! Complete each word by filling in the blank with the correct missing letter. Then place the missing letter in the corresponding numbered space above. If you choose all of the right letters, the numbered spaces will spell a nine-letter word.

___ ___ ___ ___ ___ ___ ___ ___ ___
1   2   3   4   5   6   7   8   9

1. CHAR__

2. S__AVE

3. AP__ON

4. __UITS

5. B__NCH

6. __PERA

7. TIM__D

8. FLA__K

9. __XACT

20 Lose-a-Letter

The word below can be shortened to form a new word by deleting one letter at a time, but not changing the order of the letters. For example, PAINT can be shortened to PANT to PAN to AN to A. How far can you get with STOLID?

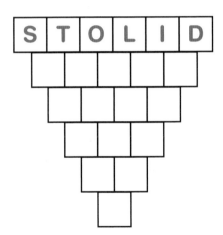

S	T	O	L	I	D

21 Switcheroo Again!

The words below have nothing in common—until you switch one letter in each word. The new words will have a common theme!

EGO _____

TEST _____

BIND _____

MATCH _____

STRING _____

* * *

22 A TV Tumble

These three words, scrambled together, will spell the name of a television personality. Can you figure out the name?

RAY WHIP FREON

_____

23 Double Take

Each line below contains a different number of different letters of the alphabet. Choose the line which you think has the greatest variety of letters.

1. ARLAAXTLVUAYRTLX

2. BJKJKOZOZQZJQJPB

3. MKMMIIINDMFDIMKI

4. RRITTVUSVWXLXRIX

5. BBBOOOAAAWWSSSBW

6. RARADURUADURRRAD

7. AAMTUWWWIKJLLLNY

8. GGGHHHBCLDFVZXXX

In each group below, the same word when added to each set of letters will form a word. Can you find the missing word for each group?

A. _____E

_____AN

_____BLE

_____POO

B. _____IC

_____LER

_____IQUE

_____ELOPE

25 More Glue Words!

A Glue Word is one that makes sense with both the first word and the last word given. For example, the Glue Word for PLAY _____ BEEF is "Ground."

A. PITCH_____LIFT

B. MOUTH_____MEAL

C. WATER _____READ

D. WORRY_____HOG

E. TYPE_____OFF

F. CHOP_____BALL

G. TEA_____DRUM

* * *

26 Alphabetically Ordered

Can you think of a place name that contains the letters k, l, m, n, o in that order? Here's a hint: You'll love the view!

Welcome to the wacky world of Clue Searches. Before you start searching the grid for words, you'll first have to use the clues given to determine the words for which you're actually searching! Once you've solved the clues, test your answers by finding and circling the words in the grid.

A. 3 POPULAR PIZZA TOPPINGS

B. GREEK GODDESS OF LOVE

C. WORLD'S LARGEST RIVER, OR WELL-KNOWN WEBSITE

D. 26.2 MILE RUN

E. GOLDEN GATE CITY

F. 3 BALLROOM DANCES

G. 4 GEOMETRIC SHAPES

```
T O S M O O R H S U M G Q
E L C R I C E M L C E C K
I Z U S A W C Y E P P E R
N Q E P I Z T I W A L T Z
O T D B N C A Z E G U I W
R A H A L E N L K N F D C
E N S M U G G A M A Z O N
P G Q B Q N L A R E L R P
P O U R A O E B S F E H A
E M A I D K T F R U N P Z
P Y R N C Z R I L I A A N
Z T E O B M A M X N C S S
N O H T A R A M O D M T W
```

28 More Word Doublets

Ready for more doublet fun? Starting with the first word, change one letter at a time so that a new word is formed. Then change one letter in the new word to form yet another new word, and so on until you have arrived at the final word. Remember, you can't change the order of the letters! (For more instructions on doublet-ing, see page 18.)

A. CAN YOU CHANGE PIG INTO STY? (IN 5 STEPS)

PIG

_____

_____

_____

_____

STY

B. TRY YOUR HAND AT TURNING PEN INTO INK (IN 5 STEPS)

PEN

_____

_____

_____

_____

INK

* * *

29 A Confused Cartoon

These three words, scrambled together, will spell the name of a famous cartoon character. Who is it?

LISTEN OFF TREND

_____

30 A Box of Chocolates?

Each clue suggests a seven-letter word beginning with P and ending in N. When you have placed all of your answers in the diagram, the seven-letter word down the middle will reveal what you might be doing with your box of chocolates!

P					N	Army unit
P					N	Model of perfection
P					N	Ardor
P					N	A share
P					N	Large, long-billed bird
P					N	He, she, or it
P					N	Bird that does not fly

Riddle

Can you take a girl's name away from a New York town and leave an ancient Roman garment?

Answer: Sara-toga

31 CryptoList: National Parks

Your travel agent suggests a family vacation to one of the National Parks. He gives you a list of his top choices. But being a funny guy, he has coded his list of National Parks so that each letter in the original text has been substituted with another. For example, T becomes A, R becomes K, etc. The same code is used throughout the entire list. Can you break the code and decide where to go this summer?

YEPQR HPQOCQ   BZCQ

OXDDCLMICQX   RXQPDZ

OCMXUZIX   PEHFXM

PHPRZP   XAXEYDPRXM

YEPQR IXICQ   RXPIF APDDXO

Each word below can be shortened to form a new word by deleting one letter at a time, but not changing the order of the letters. For example, PAINT can be shortened to PANT to PAN to AN to A. How far can you get with CREATE?

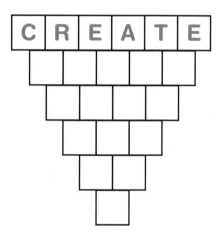

33 Switcheroo Too!

The words below have nothing in common—until you switch one letter in each word. The new words will have a common theme!

BAND _____

CATTLE _____

SAVE _____

SURE _____

SKIM _____

SHALL _____

* * *

34 On the Rocks

These three words, scrambled together, will spell the name of a classic rock star. Can you unscramble the name?

CLAMP RACY TUNE

_____

35 More Lucky Letters

Got a rabbit's foot or a four-leaf clover on hand? It might just help you solve this Lucky Letters puzzle. Complete each word by filling in the blank with the correct missing letter. Then place the missing letter in the corresponding numbered space above. If you choose all the right letters, the numbered spaces will spell a nine-letter word.

___ ___ ___ ___ ___ ___ ___ ___ ___
1 2 3 4 5 6 7 8 9

1. __ANIC

2. B__OTH

3. DAI__Y

4. LU__KY

5. PA__SE

6. S__ACE

7. B__KER

8. TWI__E

9. PURG__

36 A Ball of a Box Cross!

Have a blast with this Box Cross puzzle. Fill in the squares with letters, one letter to a square, so that when you are finished, the squares will read the same from left to right, and from top to bottom. The first words have been filled in.

O	G	R	E
G			
R			
E			

* * *

37 Letter Subtraction

Can you remove six letters from a word of nine letters and leave ten?

38 Some Doublet Dilemmas

Hone your doubleting skills with these tricky word pairs. Starting with the first word, change one letter at a time so that a new word is formed. Then change one letter in the new word to form yet another new word, and so on until you have arrived at the final word. Remember, you can't change the order of the letters! (For more instructions on doubleting, see page 18.)

A. TURN WET INTO DRY (IN 6 STEPS)

WET

_____

_____

_____

_____

_____

DRY

B. CHANGE HEAD INTO TAIL (IN 5 STEPS)

HEAD

_____

_____

_____

_____

TAIL

* * *

39 A Class-ic Problem

A group of students sat down to take their final exam. The teacher announced that the exam would be comprised of a single problem, then wrote the following on the blackboard and left the room.

YYURYYUBICURYY FOR ME.

Can you solve the problem?

A Jumble of Jocks

The letters of the following words, when rearranged, make the names of different sports. Exercise your brain with this word scramble!

FLOG

CROSCE

CHYEKO

GBNOLWI

RRAYHEC

NCMYSATGSI

LOOP

YGRUB

REALSOCS

TICCERK

LAVLBLEYLO

41 Build-a-Word Again!

Here's another brain-teasing Build-a-Word for you. Remember, each row contains the same three-letter word, though its position may change from row to row. A clue is given for each row.

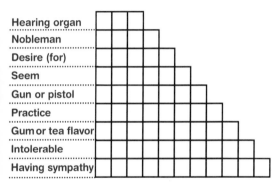

Hearing organ			
Nobleman			
Desire (for)			
Seem			
Gun or pistol			
Practice			
Gum or tea flavor			
Intolerable			
Having sympathy			

Riddle

What word is spelled incorrectly in the dictionary?

Answer: Incorrectly

42 Some Sticky Glue Words!

This Glue Word puzzle is sticky and tricky. Remember, a Glue Word is one that makes sense with both the first word and the last word given. For example, the Glue Word for PLAY _____ BEEF is "Ground."

A. GOLD_____HOUR

B. GIFT_____AROUND

C. GENE_____PARTY

D. FROST_____PLATE

E. BROWN_____PLUM

F. FAIL_____PASSAGE

G. GATE_____ROOM

43 A Boxed Set

Each clue suggests a seven-letter word beginning with C and ending in T. When you have placed all of your answers in the diagram, the seven-letter word down the middle will reveal what this box holds!

						T	Idea
						T	Type of cigar
						T	Nightclub offering
						T	Imitator
						T	Tropical fruit
						T	Join
						T	Ask the advice of

Riddle

What clothing does a house wear?

Answer: Address

44 A Wild-e Quotation

The words of this Oscar Wilde quote have gone, well, wild! Can you tame it? Place the letters in each column in one of the empty boxes directly above them. You can only use each letter once. When all of the letters have been placed correctly, a well-known Oscar Wilde quotation will read across the boxes.

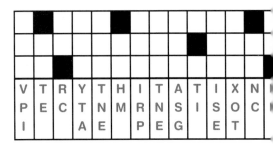

	■				■							■
								■				
		■										■
V	T	R	Y	T	H	I	T	A	T	I	X	N
P	E	C	T	N	M	R	N	S	I	S	O	C
I			A	E		P	E	G		E	T	

Riddle

What word will break if you name it?

45 The Ms Have It!

My, Mrs. Martin makes mucho money! The importance of the letter M cannot be understated. Below you'll find groups of four letters that can't do much on their own, but when you add an M to the mix, you can then create a five-letter word. (Hint: None of the five-letter words begin with M.) Here's a bonus question: Can you then form a six-letter word using the first letter of each word and an additional M?

M

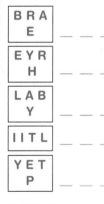

B R A E   _ _ _ _ _

E Y R H   _ _ _ _ _

L A B Y   _ _ _ _ _

I I T L   _ _ _ _ _

Y E T P   _ _ _ _ _

BONUS: _ _ _ _ _ _

The ticket broker is offering you half-price seats at a number of Broadway musicals. To get the deal, though, you'll have to decode his list. Each letter in the original text has been substituted with another. For example, T becomes A, R becomes K, etc. The same code is used throughout the entire list. You better get cracking. Curtain's up in 10 minutes!

AS BDTG EDNS

WVR FVDYWHA HB WVR HFRGD

LDWU

HPEDVHAD

QGRDUR

D LVHGZU ETYR

ATUU UDTQHY

RMTWD

UHZWV FDLTBTL

ORUW UTNR UWHGS

Each word below can be shortened to form a new word by deleting one letter at a time, but not changing the order of the letters. For example, PAINT can be shortened to PANT to PAN to AN to A. How far can you get with CLEANSER?

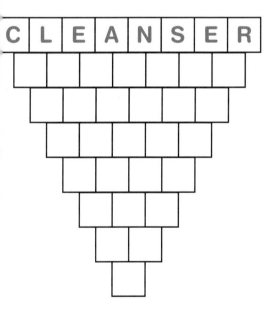

48 You Still Can't Miss!

In each group below, the same word when added to each set of letters will form a word. Can you find the missing word for each group?

A . LAV_____ER

　　R_____ER

　　TR_____Y

　　SPL_____OR

B . _____TIAL

　　_____ROT

　　_____ODY

　　_____KA

49 Splits on Ice!

Snow is falling! Unfortunately, these 12 six-letter cold weather terms have split in half. Can you pair off the groups of letters to re-form them? Each group of letters can only be used once.

STY	ARC	RRY	FLA	POW	TER
ANO	LLY	WIN	FRO	TIC	RAK
FLU	EZE	DER	ICI	DRI	KES
CLE	FTS	VEL	CHI	SHO	FRE

_____ _____   _____ _____

_____ _____   _____ _____

_____ _____   _____ _____

_____ _____   _____ _____

_____ _____   _____ _____

_____ _____   _____ _____

50 Jumble Jacks

It's time to exercise your brain with some more jumble fun. Use the 9 letters in the jumble box below to build the word that answers each clue below. Each word must incorporate the central R. If you're really on your game, you will also be able to figure out what place name includes all nine letters!

O	P	I
N	R	A
S	G	E

5 Letters
Trap
Elevate
Complain
Extra
Instrument

6 Letters
Shooter
A season
Twelfth grader

7 Letters

Areas
Public image
Harvesting
Disregards

8 Letters

More absorbent

* * *

51 A Heroic Mess

These four words, scrambled together, will spell the name of one of Hollywood's best-known action heroes. How fast can you solve this scramble?

RAZED WRENCH RAGES LONG

_____

Riddle

What is it that, after you take away the whole, some still remains?

Answer: Wholesome

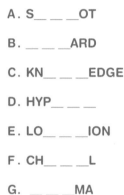 52 Confusing Creatures

The animals have gotten loose and broken down a bunch of fences, not to mention a bunch of words. Each of the words below can be repaired by placing the name of a three-letter animal in the blanks.

A. S_ _ _OT

B. _ _ _ARD

C. KN_ _ _EDGE

D. HYP_ _ _

E. LO_ _ _ION

F. CH_ _ _L

G. _ _ _MA

53 Build-a-Word Bonanza

There's nothing more diverting than a Build-a-Word puzzle. Give this one a whirl! Each row contains the same three-letter word, though its position may change from row to row. A clue is given for each row.

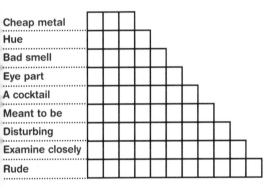

Cheap metal
Hue
Bad smell
Eye part
A cocktail
Meant to be
Disturbing
Examine closely
Rude

54 A Crafty Clue Search

Seriously, these Clue Searches just keep getting harder. Can you keep up? In the word search opposite, you'll first need to use the clues given to determine the words for which you're searching! Then find and circle the words in the grid.

A. 4 GEMSTONES

B. 5TH AMERICAN PRESIDENT

C. A PALINDROME YOU CAN PADDLE

D. 3 COLORS BEGINNING WITH THE LETTER P

E. 3 TYPES OF WINDSTORMS

```
A U M D L J I H X N U V A
F P K R C P B U C E I F P
D P E I A N G R D L C D E
D L A R E M E R K M N R A
I U L M I S Z I P E O U R
A M P S X W R C T B O I L
M S E L U D I A M O H E G
O O S F E L G N F C P N R
N P N V R A O E K A Y A K
D S I R P R U S L L T B Z
C Y C L O N E R V I E P E
Z N G B M E L P R U P J B
A W P E N K C F D N S L Y
```

55 The Luckiest Letters

So are you feeling lucky? A bit of luck will speed your solving, but ultimately, it's up to your brain! Complete each word by filling in the blank with the correct missing letter. Then place the missing letter in the corresponding numbered space above. If you choose all the right letters, the numbered spaces will spell a nine-letter word.

__ __ __ __ __ __ __ __ __
1 2 3 4 5 6 7 8 9

1. S__ORT

2. __CORN

3. WHI__S

4. PRO__E

5. __NITE

6. COLO__

7. BRIN__

8. GU__ST

9. BLU__T

56 A Wild-er Quotation

The words of this Oscar Wilde quote have gone, well, wild! Can you tame it? Place the letters in each column in one of the empty boxes directly above them. You can only use each letter once. When all of the letters have been placed correctly, a well-known Oscar Wilde quotation will read across the boxes.

I	W	G	A	S	A	L	O	T	D	B	O	B	T
G	H	T	I	S	N	N	T	H	A	H	A	B	O
T	N	E	R	O	K	E	K	E	T	B	I	U	E
U	T	O		L	E	L	D		A	N	E	N	N
				T			Y			E		I	G

Each word below can be shortened to form a new word by deleting one letter at a time, but not changing the order of the letters. For example, PAINT can be shortened to PANT to PAN to AN to A. How far can you get with SINGLET?

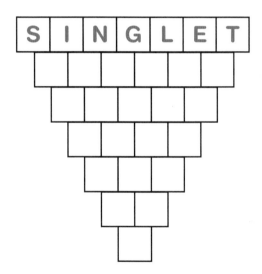

58 Do you miss me?

In each group below, the same word when added to each set of letters will form a word. Can you find the missing word for each group?

A. _____IOUS

_____RIER

_____THER

_____TIVE

B. _____K

_____CH

_____DLE

_____GLE

59 Calling All Letters

Using each letter of the alphabet just once, can you add 1 or 2 letters to each side of the letter groups below to form 11 words?

A B C D E F G H I J K L M N O P Q R S T U V W X Y Z

___UIC___   ___FOL___

___EMP___   ___RIN___

___EBR___   ___ORR___

___RES___   ___ICN___

___OKE___   ___WER___

___ENO___

* * *

60 Vowel Play

Can you think of an English word that contains all five vowels a, e, i, o, u in that order?

61 Build-a-Word Brain Buster

Here's a Build-a-Word that will build some real brain muscle! Each row contains the same three-letter word, though its position may change from row to row. A clue is given for each row.

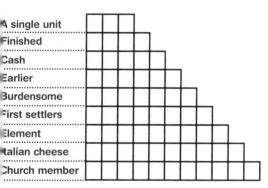

A single unit
Finished
Cash
Earlier
Burdensome
First settlers
Element
Italian cheese
Church member

65

62 Jumpin' Jumbles!

Are you ready to jumble? Use the 9 letters in the jumble box below to build the word that answers each clue below. Each word must incorporate the central P. So, are you a master jumbler? Prove you hold the highest rank in the land by finding the word that incorporates all nine letters!

D	S	R
N	P	E
T	I	E

5 Letters

Velocity

Soak in liquid

Pay out

Eyed

Primp

Disrobe

6 Letters

Arachnid

Bother

Lively intelligence

Clergyman

Elf

7 Letters

Fixed payment

Notwithstanding

Zebra-like

Snake

8 Letters

Raced

Feigns

* * *

63 A Devious Diamond

Place the letters of the fourteen-letter word ACCOMPLISHMENT in each of the spaces below to spell 2 three-letter words, 2 five-letter words and 1 seven-letter word. Each letter of ACCOMPLISHMENT will only be used once.

ACCOMPLISHMENT

```
    _ I _

  _ R _ A _

_ Y _ I _ A _

  _ N _ O _

    _ E _
```

64 SplitSplat!

The hotel's breakfast buffet is a mess! All of the dishes are split in half. Can you pair off the groups of letters to form 12 six-letter items you might find at breakfast? Each group of letters can be used only once.

MUE	NTZ	OME	PAS	CER	FLE
PES	FIN	QUI	CRE	FEE	URT
CHE	TRY	EAL	BAN	BLI	MUF
LET	WAF	COF	SLI	YOG	ANA

65 Box Cross with a Twist

Just when you think you've mastered the art of the Box Cross, we've added a twist! Fill in the squares with letters, one letter to a square, so that when you are finished, the squares will read the same from left to right, and from top to bottom—and so that the long diagonals each spell a word as well! The first words have been filled in.

B	A	S	S
A			
S			
S			

66 A Periodic Puzzler

The letters of the following words, when rearranged, make the names of different elements of the periodic table. So, how well do you remember chem class?

CRYMURE _____

NZIC _____

OBACRN _____

IONR _____

GONXEY _____

CERISAN _____

PCPREO _____

VERSLI _____

TNNOGEIR _____

DSUIMO _____

67 Shuffle, Hop, Step

These five words, scrambled together, will spell the name of one legendary dancer. This celebrity scramble should keep you on your toes!

HARK IVY OIL BASH MINK

_____

* * *

68 The Kitchen Sink

Each of the words below can be completed by placing the name of a kitchen object in the space shown.

EX_____D

IM_____ENT

OC_____Y

_____ONESTY

So you think Clue Searches are a breeze? Well, give this one a whirl and see whether or not you are a true master. In the word search opposite, you'll first need to use the clues given to determine the words for which you're searching! Then find and circle the words in the grid.

A. 4 STATES BEGINNING WITH THE LETTER M

B. 3 FIVE-LETTER WORDS BEGINNING WITH THE LETTER Q

C. 1988 OSCAR-WINNING FILM

D. 3 ARMY RANKS

E. 3 RACQUET SPORTS

```
G X C M D A I R O J A M Q
E L A O W R E L N N Q A U
P R N E U T A X U Q U I K
E K A U Q D U I M U P N A
T A T S U W Y V N P E E O
O F N A G I H C I M L F Z
U W O H A A J S Q U A S H
Q U M Y C U S S U U R N O
R B A D M I N T O N E T W
M G L C S Q U B P A N S K
O F M S I N N E T O E U T
Y N I A T P A C J H G S A
A M H V P I M F E M U C Y
```

Are you a true car aficionado? If so, you'll certainly be able to decode the following list of car makers. Each letter in the original text has been substituted with another. For example, T becomes A, R becomes K, etc. The same code is used throughout the entire list. OK, start your engines . . .

LTYYG-LTZKO

YVDWTLAJQCQ

STLGKJO

YOREG

MOLLVLQ

YVCH LTFOL

DQUGEWQGJQ

FTYXGNVAOC

UTZTUV

DOLKOHOG-WOCB

71 More Switcheroo!

The words below have nothing in common—until you switch one letter in each word. The new words will have a common theme!

HARD _____

LACE _____

TAME _____

SOUR _____

LICK _____

* * *

72 A Puzzle as Easy as A, B, C?

Can you think of an English word that contains the letters a, b, c, d, e in that order?

73 G Whiz!

You may know your p's and q's, but do you know your G's? Below you'll find groups of four letters that can't do much on their own, but when you add a G to the mix, you can then create a five-letter word. (Hint: None of the five-letter words begin with G.) Here's a bonus question: Can you then form a six-letter word using the first letter of each word and an additional G?

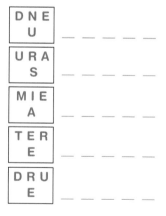

G

D N E U	_ _ _ _ _
U R A S	_ _ _ _ _
M I E A	_ _ _ _ _
T E R E	_ _ _ _ _
D R U E	_ _ _ _ _

BONUS: _ _ _ _ _ _

74 Box Cross with a Twist— Again!

Take another stab at solving a Box Cross with a Twist! Fill in the squares with letters, one letter to a square, so that when you are finished, the squares will read the same from left to right, and from top to bottom—and so that the long diagonals each spell a word as well! The first set of letters is given:

P	A	W	N
A			
W			
N			

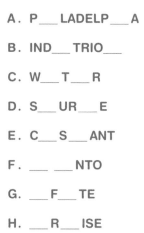 75 Double Take!

A two-letter word is missing twice in each of the words below. For example, MA__TA__ needs "IN" to make MAINTAIN. Can you solve the Double Takes below?

A. P___LADELP___A

B. IND___TRIO___

C. W___T___R

D. S___UR___E

E. C___S___ANT

F. ___ ___NTO

G. ___F___TE

H. ___R___ISE

76 Switcheroo Fun!

The words below have nothing in common—until you switch one letter in each word. The new words will have a common theme!

EYE   _____

CHEAT   _____

WHINE   _____

GROIN   _____

COIN   _____

Riddle

What has a mouth but cannot eat, what can run but never walk, and has a bed but never sleeps?

Answer: A river

77 The Wild-est Quotation

It will take a wily mind to unravel this well-known Oscar Wilde quote. Place the letters in each column in one of the empty boxes directly above them. You can only use each letter once. When all of the letters have been placed correctly, this popular Wilde quotation will read across the boxes.

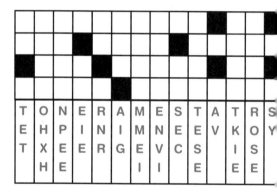

T	O	N	E	R	A	M	E	S	T	A	T	R	S
E	H	P	I	N	I	M	N	E	E	V	K	O	Y
T	X	E	E	R	G	E	V	C	S		I	S	
	H	E				I	I		E		E	E	

80

78 Swing and Miss?

In each group below, the same word when added to each set of letters will form a word. Can you find the missing word for each group?

A. _____IT

   _____EST

   _____RESS

   _____NITY

B. _____HET

   _____EL

   _____ERTY

   _____ANE

79 Doublets: Master Class

If, and only if, you are a doubleting master, will you be able to solve these devious doublets. Starting with the first word, change one letter at a time so that a new word is formed. Then change one letter in the new word to form yet another new word, and so on until you have arrived at the final word. Remember, you can't change the order of the letters! (For more instructions on doubleting, see page 18.)

A. CAN YOU MAKE WHEAT INTO BREAD? (IN 7 STEPS)

WHEAT

_____

_____

_____

_____

_____

_____

BREAD

B. NOW TURN BREAD INTO TOAST (IN 7 STEPS)

BREAD

_____

_____

_____

_____

_____

_____

TOAST

Riddle

He has one and a person has two, a citizen has three and a human being has four, a personality has five and an inhabitant of earth has six. What am I?

Answer: I'm a syllable.

80 Jumblicious!

There's nothing as satisfying as a really great jumble box. Use the 9 letters in the jumble box below to build the word that answers each clue below. Each word must incorporate the central O. Now, if you can find the word that incorporates all nine letters, you'll deserve a bouquet of flowers!

5 Letters	6 Letters
Artery	Box
Nut	Prayer singer
Gin pairing	Am unable
Egyptian city	Country
Performer	
Proportion	

7 Letters

Hold

Republic
of Yugoslavia

8 Letters

Waterproof item

* * *

81 More Matchmaking!

For each group of four words below, there is
one word that goes with all of them. Can you
find the match?

WISE, PINCH, CANDY, ARCADE

_____

OVER, DOG, NAIL, GLIDER

_____

MATE, LIST, POINT, MARK

_____

CHEAP, BOARD, ROLLER, ICE

_____

MathPlay

AS MUCH FUN AS IT MAY BE TO PLAY WITH WORDS and letters, it's just as entertaining to play with numbers. To solve the math puzzles in this section, you will need to get all of your mathematical tools out of your kit. It's time to bone up on your algebra, dust off your common sense, and perk up your powers of reasoning. A slew of artful and thorny mathematical brain games awaits— and the mysteries become a bit more mysterious as you proceed. In some of the brain games, numbers have gone missing. There are also dilemmas of digits and questions of spatial relations. Take your time as you exercise your mind in MathPlay. Many solutions reveal themselves if you give yourself the chance to really consider the problem at hand. An eraser may be helpful, too. Because if at first you don't succeed, try, try again!

❶ A Baaaa Bender

A herd of sheep and turkeys has 99 heads and feet. How many are there of each, if there are twice as many turkeys as sheep?

* * *

❷ An Even Exchange

Can you find four consecutive even integers so that the sum of the first two numbers is 22 and the last two numbers is 30?

* * *

❸ Starter Sequence

Use your powers of reasoning to find the missing numbers in each of the following sequences:

A. 3, 7, 4, 8, __ 9, 6, __

B. 1, 2, 4, 5, 7, 8, 10, __ __

C. 7, 8, 5, 6, 3, __ __ 2

4 A Checkered Puzzle

Can you place eight checkers on a checkerboard such that no two are in line horizontally, vertically, or diagonally?

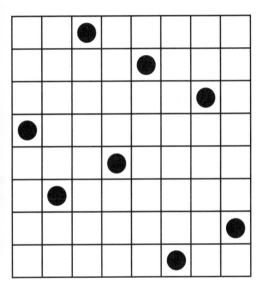

5 Tell the Number

There is a certain number, if multiplied by three-eighths of itself, the result is 96. Can you figure out the number?

* * *

6 A Starter Square

Can you fill in the empty squares so that every column and row and both diagonals add up to 34? All of the integers from 1 to 16 can only be used once.

4		14	
	6		12
5		11	
	3		13

7 A Barnyard Brainteaser

In Farmer John's barn, there are a number of spiders, goats, and ducks. There are six times as many spiders as ducks, and five times as many goats as ducks. Altogether, there are 2,100 feet. How many spiders, goats, and ducks are in the barn?

* * *

8 A Cyclical Dilemma

If you have two equal cog wheels, and one is stationary, how many turns will the other make revolving around it?

* * *

9 An Age-Old Question

Jodi is four times as old as her daughter Hannah. In 20 years, she will be twice as old as Hannah. How old are Jodi and Hannah now?

10 Triangular Magic

Here's a tricky triangle to solve. Can you arrange the digits 1, 2, 3, 4, 5, 6, 7, 8, 9 so that all three sides of the triangle add up to 19?

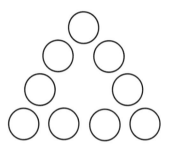

* * *

11 A Birthday Baffler

Jane had a birthday party. As she counted the candles on the cake, she remarked, "My, I'm old now! But I'm not as old as you, am I, Uncle John?" Her uncle replied with a smile, "No, you surely are not as old as I. In fact, I'm four times as old as you are, but in six more years, I will be only three times as old as you." How old is Jane now?

12 A Not So Sneaky Square

Can you place each of the digits from 1 to 9 in the grid below so that the calculations work across and down as indicated? We've given you a few numbers to help you get started!

(**Note:** In Sneaky Squares, the order of operations works from left to right, or top to bottom. For example, $8 + 6 \div 2 \rightarrow 14 \div 2 = 7$. The addition is completed before the division as it comes first.)

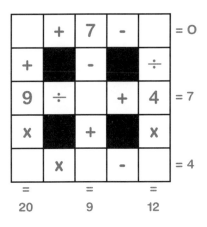

⑬ A Plethora of Nines

Can you write the number 100 with six nines?

* * *

⑭ A Simple Split?

Can you halve 11 so that it equals 6?

* * *

⑮ A Deck of Trouble

Three aces, three deuces, and three treys are laid out on a table:

A 2 3

3 A 2

2 3 A

You'll notice that the points total 6, adding across, down, or diagonally—with one exception. One diagonal adds only to three. Can you make the square add to six in all straight lines by moving only three cards?

16 A Cubic Matter

A cube measuring three inches on each side (3 x 3 x 3) is painted all over the outer surface. Then the cube is cut into one-inch cubes. How many of the smaller cubes had:

A. PAINT ON THREE SIDES ONLY

B. PAINT ON TWO SIDES ONLY

C. PAINT ON ONE SIDE ONLY

D. PAINT ON NO SIDE

* * *

17 A Series of Sequences

What's the logic behind each of these sequences? You'll have to figure that out to find the missing numbers:

A. 2, 9, 3, 8, __ __ 5, 6

B. 1, 4, 2, 8, 4, 16, __ __

C. 0, 1, 1, 2, 3, 5, 8, 13, __ __

18 A Digital Arrangement

Arrange the digits 0, 1, 2, 3, 4, 5, 6, 7, 8, 9 so that they will equal 100.

* * *

19 Tommy's Toy Run

Tommy gets a paper route and soon fills up his piggy bank. One day, he empties the bank and finds he has exactly $100. He goes to the toy store and buys exactly 100 toys. A video game costs $15, a pack of baseball cards costs $1, and a plastic dinosaur costs $.25. He buys at least one of each toy and spends all his money. How many video games, card packs, and dinosaurs does he buy?

20 Magic Square

Can you place the first nine integers, from 1 to 9 in the squares below, so that when you add the three numbers in any line, horizontal, vertical, or diagonal, you get the same total every time?

Solving Magic Squares and other Magic Shapes relies on cleverly placing numbers to create a particular sum. A strategy of trial and error will get you started, but look for patterns as you go to speed the problem solving process!

21 Another Problem of Age

When I am as old as my father is now I shall be seven times the age my son is now. By then my son will be the same age that I am now. The combined ages of my father and myself total 100 years. How old is my son?

* * *

22 Lock Box

Each of the boxes below has the same guiding principle. Can you unlock the logic of the first two boxes and so find the missing number in the last box?

2	4
6	36

9	81
1	1

3	9
10	?

23 Applesauce

John stole some apples from Farmer Smith's orchard. The farmer saw him and gave chase. When he finally caught the boy, most of the apples were gone. Farmer Smith demanded payment for the loot. John said, "I will pay you if you can tell me how many apples I took. I gave half of them away, ate two, then gave away half of the remainder. Just before you caught me I threw one apple in the creek. I have left just one-eighth of the number I took." Can you help Farmer Smith figure this out?

* * *

24 Simple Subtraction?

From 19, can you take 1 and leave 20?

* * *

25 Hog Central

Can you put nine pigs in four pens so that there will be an odd number in each pen?

26 Warning! An Addition Problem

Each of the letters below represents a different digit. To solve this letter addition, you'll first need to form a sentence of three words with the nine letters shown below. Next, number the letters consecutively in the order in which they occur in the sentence. You can then work out the addition, substituting the numbers for letters.

```
          B
      O   E
      U   N
      G   D
  +   A   R
  ─────────
  E   O   N
```

27 Coin Sorter

A man has $1.15 in six coins. He cannot make change for a dollar, a half dollar, a quarter, a dime, or a nickel. What coins does he have?

* * *

28 A Beach Build

Sandy is at the beach and decides to build a sand castle shaped like a pyramid. Sandy only has one small bucket at her disposal. She fills the bucket with wet sand and upends it to create a cylinder. The square base of her pyramid is 8 cylinders long by 8 cylinders wide. How many times will Sandy have to fill her bucket with sand to build her sand pyramid?

Can you start at "A" and move in such a way as to touch every square and return to "A" in twelve straight moves? You may move horizontally, vertically, or diagonally and go as far as the limits of the board will allow.

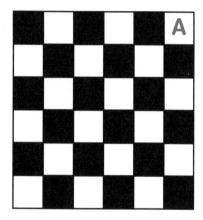

30 Tommy's Tangle

When Tommy opens up his piggy bank, he finds that he has just 100 coins in half dollars, pennies, and dimes. When he counted his money, he found that he had exactly $5.00. How many coins did Tommy have of each denomination?

✳ ✳ ✳

31 A Little More Triangular Magic

Can you arrange the digits 1, 2, 3, 4, 5, 6, 7, 8, 9 so that all three sides of the triangle add up to 20?

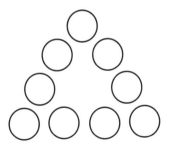

32 Mixed-Up Dominoes

The dominoes have fallen out of their special box. Luckily, the numbers were written on the bottom of the box. Can you put all twelve dominoes back in their 4 x 6 box so that they fit perfectly?

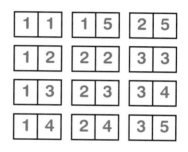

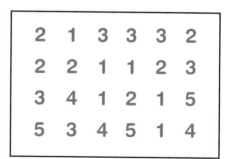

33 Another Sneaky Square

Can you place each of the digits from 1 to 9 in the grid below so that the calculations work across and down as indicated? We've given you a start!

(**Note:** In Sneaky Squares, the order of operations works from left to right, or top to bottom. For example, $8 + 6 \div 2 \rightarrow 14 \div 2 = 7$. The addition is completed before the division as it comes first.)

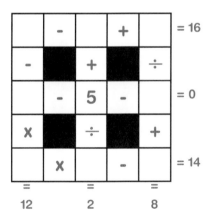

34 The Confused Commuter

Mike overslept and hit rush hour traffic on his drive to work one morning and averaged only 30 miles per hour. At the end of the day, Mike left early and returned home along the exact same route and averaged 45 miles per hour. If Mike spent a total of one hour commuting to and from work, how many miles is it from Mike's house to his office?

* * *

35 The Square Doughnut

Can you arrange the numbers 1, 2, 3, 4, 5, 6, 7, 8, 9, 10, 11, 12 so that each side of the square adds up to 27?

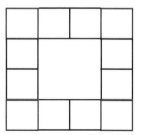

36 Another Lock Box

Each of the boxes below has the same guiding principle. Can you unlock the logic of the first two boxes and so find the missing number in the last box?

6	10
20	3

9	8
1	72

4	13
2	?

* * *

37 Some Serious Sequences

To find the missing terms in these sequences, you will have to employ all your reasoning skills!

A. J, F, M, A, M, J, J, A, __ __

B. 1, 3, 6, 10, 15, __ __

C. 3, 4, 8, 9, 18, 19, __ __

Can you arrange the digits 1, 2, 3, 4, 5, 6, 7, 8, 9 so that the horizontal line and the vertical line add up to 27?

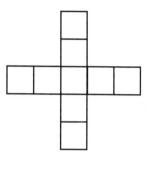

* * *

39 A Fishy Question

A fish is 15 inches long. The head is as long as the tail. If the head were twice as long, the head and tail would be as long as the body. How long is each?

40 Puzzling in Peoria

John Pokey set out from Pottstown one morning to drive to Peoria, where he had a business appointment. Presently he figured that he would be late if he did not speed up. He had been on the road for 36 minutes, averaging 30 miles per hour. At that rate, he would be 16 minutes late for his appointment. So he stepped on the gas, and by averaging 35 miles per hour for the rest of the trip he just made Peoria in time. How far is it from Pottstown to Peoria?

* * *

41 A Field of Possibilities

A square field with a fence around it contains 16 acres. It is divided into squares of an acre each. How many subdivisions are:

A. FENCED ON TWO SIDES?

B. FENCED ON ONE SIDE ONLY?

C. FENCED ON NO SIDE?

42 A Dilemma of Dominoes

Can you fit all of the 15 dominoes below into
the 5 x 6 grid?

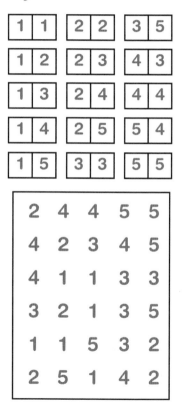

1	1	2	2	3	5
1	2	2	3	4	3
1	3	2	4	4	4
1	4	2	5	5	4
1	5	3	3	5	5

2	4	4	5	5
4	2	3	4	5
4	1	1	3	3
3	2	1	3	5
1	1	5	3	2
2	5	1	4	2

43 Lock Box Again

All of the boxes below have something in common. Can you unlock the logic of the first two boxes and so find the missing number in the last box?

2	7
15	25

30	12
4	3

19	11
10	?

* * *

44 Another Fishy Question

A fisherman caught a fish and was asked how long it was. He replied, "It is 20 inches plus half its length." How long was the fish?

* * *

45 Additional Arrangements

Arrange the digits 1, 2, 3, 4, 5, 6, 7 so that when the numbers are added up, they will total 100.

46 Making More Magic!

Can you place the integers from 1 to 25 in the squares below, so that the sum of the five numbers in any line—horizontal, vertical, or diagonal—is 65? (We've placed several numbers to get you started!)

17				
			14	
		13		22
10			21	
	18			

* * *

47 The Missing Number

In the set of numbers below, there is one more two-digit number that should be included. Do you know what it is?

16, 52, 25, 34, 70, 61, ___

48 The Lady and the Eggs

A shopkeeper asked a lady how many eggs she delivered. She replied, "I do not remember, but when counted 2, 3, 4, 5, or 6 at a time, always one remained. Counted 7 at a time, they came out even." What were the fewest number of eggs that could have been delivered?

* * *

49 A Head Full of Numbers

How quickly can you solve the problem below?

0+0+1-1+2-2+3-3+4-4+5-5+6-6+7-7+8-

8+9-9+10-10+11-11+12-12+13-13+14-14+15-

15+16-16+17-17+18-18+19-19+20-20+21-

21+22-22+23-23+24-24+25-25= ?

50 A Puzzling Playgroup

Little Peetie is going to his playgroup. He has a bag of marbles which his mother says he must share if he wants to bring them to playgroup. When he tries to give each of his friends 5 marbles, one child will only end up with 4, and Peetie will have none for himself, but if he tries to give each of his friends 4 marbles, he ends up with 12 spare marbles for himself. How many marbles are in the bag and how many friends are in Peetie's playgroup?

* * *

51 Triple Play

I have three of the same digits. Added together they make 24. The digit is not 8. What is it?

52 A Super Sneaky Square

A Sneaky Square may look easy, but it takes a sharp mind to solve. Can you place each of the digits from 1 to 9 in the grid below so that the calculations work across and down as indicated?

(**Note:** In Sneaky Squares, the order of operations works from left to right, or top to bottom. For example, $8 + 6 \div 2 \rightarrow 14 \div 2 = 7$. The addition is completed before the division as it comes first.)

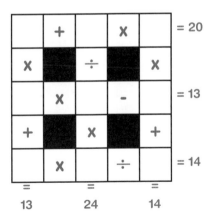

53 A Money Issue

Each letter represents a different digit. Can you decipher the following so that it makes a correct addition problem?

       S E N D

+   M O R E

M O N E Y

* * *

54 A Dastardly Criss Cross

Can you arrange the digits 1, 2, 3, 4, 5, 6, 7, 8, 9 so that not only do the horizontal line and the vertical line add up to 24, but that the four bolded squares also add up to 24?

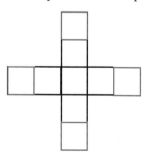

55 The Growing Tree

Morgan and Tommy have been lifelong friends. When they graduated from high school, they carved their initials on a tree trunk 4 feet off the ground. Exactly one year later, they came home from college. The tree had grown 6 inches. During the following years, the tree doubled the amount it grew each year. How high were their initials on their tenth reunion?

* * *

56 A Tricky Lock Box

Each of the boxes below has something in common. Can you unlock the logic of the first two boxes and so find the missing number in the last box?

14	22
5	13

15	1
19	5

9	11
3	?

57 Sequences: Master Class

These scheming sequences are not easy to solve. Prove yourself the Master of the Sequence and find the missing terms!

A. 84, 52, 42, 34, 22, __

B. 6, 24, 60, 120, 210, 336, __

C. 1, 11, 21, 1211, 111221, __

* * *

58 A Puzzle of Pies

Penny the Pie Maker is off to sell her pies at market. She has to travel through 5 towns on her way, but at each town, the tax collector demands half her pies as an entrance fee. However, the tax collectors are not all bad fellows. Each one gives Penny back a single pie. So, how many pies does Penny have to leave her kitchen with to make sure she arrives at market with exactly two pies?

59 A Trickier Challenge

Can you arrange these five digits 1, 2, 3, 4, 5 so that the first two digits multiplied by the middle digit will produce the last two digits?

* * *

60 Too Much Wine?

Two men are in the cellar and find an 8-gallon cask full of wine, an empty 5-gallon cask, and an empty 3-gallon cask. They wish to measure out two lots of four gallons each. How can it be accomplished?

* * *

61 Serious about Cereal

The local supermarket is running a promotion. For every 5 cereal box tops you redeem, you receive a new box of cereal. Now, Robin loves cereal so she collects 81 box tops from her friends and family. How many boxes of cereal will Robin get to eat in total?

62 The Sneakiest Square

So you think you can out-sneak the Sneaky Square? Good luck. This Sneaky Square is downright devious! Place each of the digits from 1 to 9 in the grid below so that the calculations work across and down as indicated!

(**Note:** In Sneaky Squares, the order of operations works from left to right, or top to bottom. For example, $8 + 6 \div 2 \rightarrow 14 \div 2 = 7$. The addition is completed before the division as it comes first.)

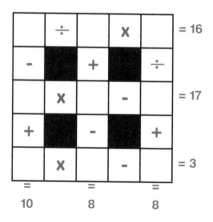

63 A Dastardly Doughnut

Can you arrange the numbers 1, 2, 3, 4, 5, 6, 7, 8, 9, 10, 11, 12 so that not only does each side of the square add up to 26, but that the four corners also add up to 26?

Riddle

What grows larger the more you take from it?

64 Cracking the Combination

Using the numbers 1, 2, 3, 4, and 5, you can make any number from 1 to 15 by simply adding them in proper combinations, as follows: The original digits supply 1 to 5, then you can make the numbers 6 through 15 thus:

$1 + 5 = 6$ $2 + 4 + 5 = 11$

$2 + 5 = 7$ $3 + 4 + 5 = 12$

$3 + 5 = 8$ $1 + 3 + 4 + 5 = 13$

$4 + 5 = 9$ $2 + 3 + 4 + 5 = 14$

$1 + 4 + 5 = 10$ $1 + 2 + 3 + 4 + 5 = 15$

Now, name five numbers which will enable you to obtain any number from 1 to 30 by adding them in different combinations?

65 A Poker Puzzle

The five members of a poker club meet every Saturday night to play stud poker. They play at a round table, and in every session they sit down to a different order. They would not count it a new arrangement if the players should all move one chair to the left or right, keeping their sequence around the table the same. After they have exhausted all possible sequences, they hold a banquet, and on the following week, they begin all over again. How many weeks elapse from one banquet to the next?

Riddle

Amy picked a book off the highest shelf in her room. On the spine she read "How to Jog." She ran out of the room and opened the book but found it had absolutely nothing to do with jogging. What was the book about?

66 Not-So-Simple Division

Can you decipher the following long division problem? Each letter stands for a different digit.

```
                U U M
        ┌─────────────
H D M ) R R T G B
          E M H
        ───────
          K U K G
          E M H
        ───────
            D D B B
            D G T R
          ───────
            D G M
```

67 Wayne's Watch

One evening, Wayne notices that his watch has stopped—again! He forgets to re-set it until the following afternoon, at which point he asks his wife what time it is. His wife is so annoyed that he still hasn't fixed his watch that she answers, "The time now is the sum of 1/3 of the time since noon today and 1/6 of the time until 6 PM tonight." Wayne then sets his watch to the correct time. What time is it?

Riddle

If you have two coins that add up to 55 cents, and one of the coins isn't a half dollar, what are the coins?

Answer: A half dollar and a nickel. The coin that isn't the half dollar is the nickel, and the other coin is the half dollar.

ALL GAMES INVOLVE STRATEGIC THINKING, BUT logic games are a special breed of fun that require you to apply all of the deductive reasoning skills you have at your disposal. You may also find that those reasoning muscles get stronger as you exercise them!

In each of these brainy bafflers, you will have to draw conclusions based on the information provided. However, you may need to look beyond the obvious to formulate those conclusions! Pay close attention to the questions themselves and give yourself time to really consider each problem. Sketching the problem may prove helpful and, in some cases, a systematic approach is best. So in certain games, we've provided a grid to help you organize your conclusions. With a grid, you can eliminate possibilities one by one until you have reached the logical solution.

But if all else fails, step away from the box. Step far, far away from the box! To solve some enigmas, you'll need to put your usual logic aside and think outside the box. All of the solutions are indeed logical, but how you get there will take some creative thinking.

As you move through the LogicPlay section, the puzzles generally become more challenging. Don't let that deter you from trying the later logic games. After all, those logic puzzles are often the most diverting and entertaining!

* * *

1 Tricky Train Travel

Two trains travel nonstop from Applesburg to Bananaville every day on the same track at the same speed. One train takes an hour and 10 minutes and the other train takes 70 minutes. Why is that?

* * *

2 Riddle for the Ages

I have no brothers or sisters, yet the father of that man is my father's son. What relation is he to me?

3 A Calculating Conundrum

If a fourth of forty is six, what is a third of 20?

* * *

4 A River Runs Through It

A farmer going to market has a fox, a goose, and a basket of corn. He comes to a river, but the boat will only carry the farmer and one of his charges. Now, if he leaves the fox and the goose alone, the fox will eat the goose, and if he leaves the goose and corn alone, the goose will eat the corn. How can he safely take them all across the river?

* * *

5 Udderly Puzzling?

A boy, herding some cows, was asked how many cows he had. He said, "When they are in line there are two cows ahead of a cow, two cows behind a cow, and one cow in the middle." How many cows did he have?

6 All in a Day's Work

Alice, Betty, and Charlene are a banker, an editor, and a chef. The chef, who is an only child, is the shortest. Charlene, who is married to Alice's brother, is taller than the editor. What is each woman's job?

	ALICE	BETTY	CHARLENE
BANKER			
EDITOR			
CHEF			

* * *

7 Disorganized Dishes!

A cabinet contains 8 blue dishes and 8 yellow dishes that are all mixed up. Without peeking, what is the fewest number of dishes you can take from the cabinet and be certain that you have a pair of dishes the same color?

8 Montezuma's Muddle

A big Aztec and a little Aztec were walking down the path. The little Aztec was the son of the big Aztec, yet the big Aztec was not the father of the little Aztec. Why?

* * *

9 The Puzzling Penthouse

A man lives in the penthouse of a skyscraper. Every morning, he rides the elevator down to the ground floor to go to work. On his way home every evening, though, he can only ride the elevator half of the distance up the building and then has to walk the rest of the way up—except if it's raining! How can this be?

* * *

10 Double Trouble

A mother has two daughters born on the same day of the same year, but the girls are not twins. How can this be?

⑪ A Family Matter

Suzanne, John, and Larry have red, brown, and blond hair and are 11, 14, and 15 years old. The youngest has blond hair. John is older than Larry. John does not have red hair and Larry does not have blond hair. Based on these facts, can you determine the hair color and age of each child?

	SUZANNE	JOHN	LARRY
HAIR COLOR			
AGE			

* * *

⑫ It's in the Bag!

Two mothers and two daughters went shopping. Each bought exactly one dress and yet there were only three dresses in the bag. Why?

13 A Dirty Dilemma

How much dirt is there in a hole 18 inches square and 1 foot deep?

* * *

14 Think Before You Leap

A frog, at the bottom of a 40-foot well, every day jumps up three feet and at night falls back two. How many days will it take him to get out of the well?

* * *

15 The Cider Barrel

When Jimmy wanted to buy a barrel of cider from Farmer Brown, the farmer had left only about half a barrel. Jimmy looked into the barrel and thought it was less than half full, while the farmer thought it was more than half full. They settled the matter quickly and accurately without using a measuring rod of any kind or putting anything into the barrel. How did they do it?

16 My Three Sons

An addled mother is asked the height of her three sons. She responds, saying that Alex is the shortest unless Ben is, and that if Craig isn't the shortest, then Alex is the tallest. Who is the tallest and who is the shortest?

	ALEX	BEN	CRAIG
TALLEST			
MIDDLE			
SHORTEST			

* * *

17 On Board!

New York and Philadelphia are 90 miles apart. A train leaves New York traveling at 60 miles per hour; another leaves Philadelphia at the same time traveling at 50 miles per hour. Which will be further from New York when they meet?

18 A Space Odyssey

The chief American astronaut wishes to travel from his space station to the Russian space station. It takes 6 hours to cross to the Russian station in a jet pack, but one astronaut can only carry enough oxygen for four hours. What is the fewest number of other astronauts required to help carry enough oxygen for the chief to cross—and for every astronaut to remain safe?

* * *

19 A Marital Mystery

A man shoots his wife. Then he holds her underwater for several minutes. Finally, he hangs her. An hour later, the man and his wife go out to the movies. How can this be?

20 The Mixed-up Florist

It's Valentine's Day and the flower shop is hopping. Unfortunately for the florist, his new assistant can't quite keep all the orders straight. One of the shop's best customers, Mr. Smith, had ordered three different bouquets: one for his wife, one for his sister, and one for his mother. Can you help the assistant keep his job and sort out which bouquet is meant for whom based on the statements below:

(1) If his sister received the roses, then his wife received the carnations.
(2) If his mother received the carnations, then his sister received the roses.
(3) If his mother received the lilies, then his sister received the carnations.
(4) If his mother received the roses, then his wife received the lilies.
(5) If his wife received the roses, then his sister received the lilies.

	WIFE	SISTER	MOTHER
ROSES			
CARNATIONS			
LILIES			

21 The Man of the Family

A man has three sons, and each of his sons has three sons. One man and his father constitute a "father and son" pair, as does the same man and his son. In other words, any one person may figure in any number of pairs, so long as he is paired with a different person each time. Knowing this, answer the following:

a. How many pairs of cousins are there?
b. How many pairs of father and son?
c. How many pairs of brothers?
d. How many pairs of uncle and nephew?
e. How many pairs of grandfather and grandson?

* * *

22 A Leap of Logic

A man stared through the filthy, soot-smeared window on the 30th floor of a sky-scraper. Terribly depressed, he opened the window and jumped through it. However, he was completely unscathed on landing, though there was nothing to break his fall or slow his descent. How can this be?

23 Another Leap of Logic

Rob jumps out of a plane without a parachute or any other type of flotation device, but he does not get hurt. How can this be?

* * *

24 A Dinner Cruise?

Three anthropologists and three cannibals come to a river that they must cross. The boat they have will only carry two people. All the anthropologists can row, but only one cannibal can—Cannibal YumYum. The trips must be arranged so that the cannibals never outnumber the anthropologists. In other words, one anthropologist must never be left with two cannibals or two anthropologists with the three cannibals. They were all able to get across, but how was it done?

Tommy and Jane are playing a game. Tommy has six shapes ♦ ▲ ■ ● ♣ ❤ and he has placed four of them behind the green squares. Each time Jane guesses which four shapes Tommy has chosen, he indicates how many of her guesses are the correct shape (1st column) and of those, how many are in the correct position as well (2nd column). Based on Jane's guesses below, can you solve the secret pattern?

				SHAPE	PLACE
♣	■	▲	❤	2	2
■	♣	▲	❤	2	1
♣	❤	●	■	2	1
●	♦	❤	■	2	1
♦	▲	●	■	3	0

26 Frank, Connor, and Slick

Meet a trio of unlikely friends: Frank, Connor, and Slick. Frank is aptly named for he is always frank and tells the truth. Connor, however, is the ultimate con artist. He always lies. And then there is Slick. Depending on the situation, Slick sometimes lies and sometimes tells the truth.

In the puzzles below, each of the trio makes one statement. Based on what you know about their truth-telling abilities, can you tell who is who? Each puzzle has only one solution!

I. A says: I am Frank.
   B says: I am Connor.
   C says: B is not Frank.

II. A says: I am Frank.
    B says: I am not Slick.
    C says: I am Connor.

III. A says: I am Connor!
     B says: A is Connor!
     C says: B is Connor!

IV. A says: I am not Slick.
     B says: I am Connor.
     C says: A is Slick!

V.   A says: I am not Slick.
     B says: A is Frank!
     C says: A is not Connor.

VI. A says: C is Slick
     B says: C is not Connor.
     C says: B is not Connor!

VII. A says: B is Connor!
     B says: C is Slick!
     C says: A is Frank!

VIII. A says: B is Slick!
      B says: C is Slick!
      C says: B is definitely Slick.

27 A Clubby Affair

A banker, a dentist, a doctor, and a lawyer were all members of the same country club. Their names (not necessarily respectively) were Jim, Jack, Joe, and Jerry.

1. Although they were clubmates, Jim and the dentist were not on speaking terms with Joe.
2. Jack and the lawyer were good friends.
3. Joe and the doctor lived in the same neighborhood.
4. The banker was on excellent terms with Jerry and the lawyer.

Based on the statements above, can you determine the profession of each man?

	JIM	JACK	JOE	JERRY
BANKER				
DENTIST				
DOCTOR				
LAWYER				

28 A Revolutionary Problem

During the French Revolution, Robespierre became the head of the tribunal, and was invested with extraordinary power, which enabled him to pass sentence of death upon anyone who, in his opinion, was an enemy of the state.

Robespierre immediately sent to the guillotine all persons whom he considered to be such enemies.

He was attacked by those who opposed him in the National Convention. They said he had constantly identified his own enemies with those of the state, and in this manner he had disposed of all persons against whom he had personal grievances and all persons who were likely to disagree with his policies.

Robespierre replied to the charges made by his enemies, and gave them a logical proof that the statement they made was incorrect; that any one who thus attacked him was actually *denying* the charge. What was Robespierre's argument?

29 Sibling Logic

A man and his sister were together. The man pointed across the street to a boy and said, "That boy is my nephew." The woman replied, "He is not my nephew." Can you explain this?

* * *

30 A Picnic Poser

Samantha went to her class picnic and drank some lemonade from a punch bowl that had just been set out on the table. She then left. All of the others at the picnic who drank lemonade from the punch bowl later got sick. Why didn't Samantha get sick?

31 A Cook's Conundrum

In preparing for a big holiday party, much baking had to be done. One of the following statements must be true:

(1) All of the Cook's cakes were prepared by the local bakery.
(2) Some of the Cook's cakes were prepared by the local bakery.
(3) Some of the Cook's cakes were not prepared by the local bakery.

We do not know which of these statements is true. However, which pair of statements may both be true, but cannot both be false? AND—which pair of statements may both be false, but cannot both be true?

Five neighbors decide to paint each of their houses. They all have their houses painted a different color and by a different painter. From the statements below, can you figure out which color and painter each neighbor used, and in what order the houses were painted?

Neighbors: Mr. Smith, Mr. Jones, Mr. Miller, Mrs. Roberts, Mrs. Bennett

Painters: Paul, Charlie, Henry, Matt, Aaron

Colors: Brown, Yellow, White, Red, Green

A. Mrs. Bennett's house was not painted first.
B. Charlie paints one of the houses brown.
C. Mrs. Roberts' house was painted yellow, but not by Matt.
D. Paul painted Mr. Smith's house.
E. The brown house was not painted second.
F. The green house was painted last.
G. Matt painted the fourth house, but he did not paint it white.
H. Mr. Miller's house was painted third, but by neither Charlie nor Henry.

	1ST	2ND	3RD	4TH	5TH
NEIGHBOR					
PAINTER					
COLOR					

33 A Family Dilemma

A few weeks after the birth of her daughter, Mrs. Ellis invited all of her surviving relatives to the christening. In reporting this gala event, the town newspaper remarked that there were present "two fathers and two mothers, one grandmother and three grandchildren, two sons and two daughters, one brother and two sisters, a father-in-law, a mother-in-law, and a daughter-in-law, as well as four children."

Mrs. Ellis wrote the editor at once to tell him he was mistaken. Besides the Pastor, there had not been 23 people present, but rather seven. The editor replied that he had made no mis-statement. How was that possible?

34 Code Cracker Rematch

Tommy and Jane are playing again in a Crack the Code rematch. Tommy has six shapes ♦ ▲ ■ ● ♣ ♥ and he has placed four of them behind the green squares. Each time Jane guesses which four shapes Tommy has chosen, he indicates how many of her guesses are the correct shape (1st column) and, of those, how many are in the correct position as well (2nd column). Based on Jane's guesses below, can you crack the secret pattern?

				SHAPE	PLACE
♥	■	♦	♣	3	1
♥	▲	●	♦	2	0
♦	♥	●	♣	3	2
▲	♥	■	●	2	1
♥	♦	▲	■	2	0

149

35 The Sultan's Choice

The Sultan once needed a man of great intelligence for an important mission. Unable to choose from among his three brightest courtiers, he summoned them and had them blindfolded. Then he put a skullcap on each and said: "Each of you now wears either a black or white skullcap. When I remove the blindfolds, raise your hand as soon as you see a black skullcap. Drop your hand as soon as you know the color of your own cap."

The blindfolds removed, all raised their hands at once, for the wily Sultan had put a black cap on each courtier's head. After a few minutes one courtier dropped his hand and said, "My cap is black." By what logical reasoning could he tell?

36 The Courtiers Choose Again!

The Sultan once again needed a man of great intelligence for yet another important mission. He summoned three courtiers and lined them up in a row, all facing the same direction. The courtier in the back could see the two men in front of him. The courtier in the middle could only see the first man, and the courtier in front could see no one.

The sultan told the three courtiers that he had three black caps and two white caps in all. He placed a cap on each of the courtiers' heads without the men seeing which two caps were left over. The courtier in back was asked if he could deduce what color cap he had on, but he said he could not. Then, the courtier in the middle was asked if he could deduce what color cap he had on, and he too said he could not. But then the courtier in the front, having heard both the previous answers, correctly deduced the color cap he was wearing. What color was it and by what logical reasoning could he tell?

37 A Puzzle of a Panel

Professor Rotskoffsky is planning a panel discussion on child-rearing during the 1970s. She has invited eight guests to speak, but seating arrangements are always tricky among academics. Based on the facts below, can you determine where each of the speakers sat?

Speakers: Caren Caravan, Cindy City, Leah Laptop, Lori Literati, Michele Mosaic, Rob Runner, Rich Riddle, and Dr. S. Squeeze

1. No speaker is next to another speaker with the same initials.

2. Rich Riddle, Ph.D., does not sit in the last seat, and Leah Laptop does not sit in the first seat.

3. Michele Mosaic, Ph.D., sits three seats to the left of Dr. S. Squeeze but she does not sit in the first seat.

4. Dr. Lori Literati sits four seats to the right of Ms. Caren Caravan and sits to the left of another speaker who is not Ms. Cindy City.

5. Dr. Rob Runner sits two seats to the right of Professor Leah Laptop and two seats to the left of Ms. Cindy City.

	1ST	2ND	3RD	4TH	5TH	6TH	7TH	8TH
CAREN CARAVAN								
CINDY CITY								
LEAH LAPTOP								
LORI LITERATI								
MICHELE MOSAIC								
ROB RUNNER								
RICH RIDDLE								
S. SQUEEZE								

Answers

WordPlay Answer Section

1.The Glue Word!
A. Toe, B. Roll, C. Place, D. Brow, E. Run, F. Bed, G. Intelligence

2. A Simple Scramble
Just one word. The letters of these three words are merely scrambled.

3. Missing States
Virginia, Mississippi, Tennessee, Alabama, Illinois, Ohio, Colorado, Oregon, Alaska

4. Opposites Attract
A. Formal, Relaxed; B. Lively, Dull; C. Prone, Erect; D. Common, Scarce; E. Wide, Narrow; F. Budding, Withered; G. Ace, Novice; H. Weighty, Shallow; I. Crest, Bottom

5. A Proverbial Poser
Slow and steady wins the race.

6. A 5-Star Word
There: The, Here, Her, He, Ere

7. Letter by Letter

8. A Puzzle of a President

Theodore Roosevelt

9. Switcheroo!

Theme — Halloween: Orange, Treat, Trick, Pumpkin, Mask, Witch

10. LCNS PLT Games

Accelerate, Giddy-up, Excuse me, Tomato, Intense, Enthusiast, Bond trader, What are you waiting for?, Detour, Attention!, Surfer girl, Photographer, I'm in love, One in a million, Aviator.

11. The Mystery Box

S	T	A	P	L	E	R	An office tool
S	W	E	A	T	E	R	A knitted garment
S	L	E	N	D	E	R	Thin
S	O	L	D	I	E	R	One who serves in the army
S	C	H	O	L	A	R	An academic
S	H	O	R	T	E	R	Not as tall
S	E	N	A	T	O	R	Elected representative

12. Doublets: An Introduction

Other solutions are possible.
A. DOG, COG, COT, CAT
B. TEA, PEA, PET, POT, HOT

13. An International Mix-Up

Sweden, Germany, Switzerland, Bolivia, Holland, Venezuela, China, Russia, Poland, Mexico, Denmark, France, Morocco

14. CryptoList: Ice Cream Flavors

Butter pecan, Strawberry, Neapolitan, Chocolate chip, French vanilla, Cookies and cream, Praline pecan, Cherry, Coffee, Rocky road

15. Build-a-Word Starter Set

Play a role	A	C	T								
A truth	F	A	C	T							
Desert plants	C	A	C	T	I						
Existing in fact	A	C	T	U	A	L					
Farm vehicle	T	R	A	C	T	O	R				
Break, as a rib	F	R	A	C	T	U	R	E			
Moral quality	C	H	A	R	A	C	T	E	R		
Cave hanging	S	T	A	L	A	C	T	I	T	E	
Hard to manage	I	N	T	R	A	C	T	A	B	L	E

16. Box Cross

There are several possible solutions.

F	L	O	P
L	I	V	E
O	V	E	R
P	E	R	T

M	E	A	N
E	D	G	E
A	G	E	S
N	E	S	T

17. Jumble Gym!

5 Letters: steed, stare, tress, crate, trade

6 Letters: scared, recess, secret

7 Letters: dessert, created, sedates

8 Letters: caressed

9 Letters: Descartes

18. Matchmaker, Matchmaker!

A. Open, B. Stone, C. Time, D. Water

19. Lucky Letters

TURQUOISE: 1. chart, 2. suave, 3. apron, 4. quits, 5. bunch, 6. opera, 7. timid, 8. flask, 9. exact

20. Lose-a-Letter

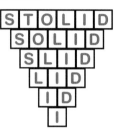

21. Switcheroo Again!

Theme = Robin: Egg, Nest, Bird, Hatch, Spring

22. A TV Tumble

Oprah Winfrey

23. Double Take

Line (7) has eleven different letters; Line (8) has ten different letters; Line (4) has nine different letters; Line (1) has eight different letters; Line (2) has seven different letters; Line (3) has six different letters; Line (5) has five different letters; and Line (6) has four different letters.

24. You Can't Miss!

A. Sham, B. Ant

25. More Glue Words!

A. Fork, B. Piece, C. Proof, D. Wart, E. Face, F. Stick, G. Kettle

26. Alphabetically Ordered

Kilimanjaro

27. No Ordinary Word Search!

A. 3 popular pizza toppings: pepperoni, sausage, mushrooms

B. Greek goddess of love: Aphrodite

C. World's largest river or well-known website: Amazon

D. 26.2 mile run: marathon

E. Golden Gate City: San Francisco

F. Three ballroom dances: mambo, tango, waltz

G. 4 geometric shapes: circle, square, triangle, rectangle

28. More Word Doublets

Other solutions are possible.

A. PIG, BIG, BAG, SAG, SAY, STY

B. PEN, TEN, TON, ION, INN, INK

29. A Confused Cartoon

Fred Flintstone

30. A Box of Chocolates?

P	L	A	T	O	O	N	Army unit
P	A	R	A	G	O	N	Model of perfection
P	A	S	S	I	O	N	Ardor
P	O	R	T	I	O	N	A share
P	E	L	I	C	A	N	Large, long-billed bird
P	R	O	N	O	U	N	He, she, or it
P	E	N	G	U	I	N	Bird that does not fly

31. CryptoList: National Parks

Grand Canyon, Yellowstone, Yosemite, Acadia, Grand Teton, Zion, Denali, Arches, Everglades, Death Valley

32. Letter by Letter Fun

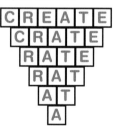

33. Switcheroo Too!

Theme = Seashore: Sand, Castle, Wave, Surf, Swim, Shell

34. On the Rocks

Paul McCartney

35. More Lucky Letters

PORCUPINE: 1. panic, 2. booth, 3. dairy, 4. lucky, 5. pause,
6. space, 7. biker, 8. twine, 9. purge

36. A Ball of a Box Cross!

There are several solutions. Here is one:

O	G	R	E
G	L	A	D
R	A	I	D
E	D	D	Y

37. Letter Subtraction

Answer: Tenacious. Remove "acious" and you have "ten" left!

38. Some Doublet Dilemmas

Other solutions are possible.

A. WET, SET, SAT, SAY, WAY, WRY, DRY
B. HEAD, HEAL, TEAL, TELL, TALL, TAIL

39. A Class-ic Problem

Too wise you are, too wise you be, I see you are too wise for me.

40. A Jumble of Jocks

Golf, Soccer, Hockey, Bowling, Archery, Gymnastics, Polo, Rugby,
Lacrosse, Cricket, Volleyball

41. Build-a-Word Again!

Hearing organ	E	A	R								
Nobleman	E	A	R	L							
Desire (for)	Y	E	A	R	N						
Seem	A	P	P	E	A	R					
Gun or pistol	F	I	R	E	A	R	M				
Practice	R	E	H	E	A	R	S	E			
Gum or tea flavor	S	P	E	A	R	M	I	N	T		
Intolerable	U	N	B	E	A	R	A	B	L	E	
Having sympathy	K	I	N	D	H	E	A	R	T	E	D

42. Some Sticky Glue Words!

A. Rush, B. Wrap, C. Pool, D. Bite, E. Sugar, F. Safe, G. Leg

43. A Boxed Set

C	O	N	C	E	P	T	Idea
C	H	E	R	O	O	T	Type of cigar
C	A	B	A	R	E	T	Nightclub offering
C	O	P	Y	C	A	T	Imitator
C	O	C	O	N	U	T	Tropical fruit
C	O	N	N	E	C	T	Join
C	O	N	S	U	L	T	Ask the advice of

44. A Wild-e Quotation

I can resist everything except temptation.

45. The Ms Have It!

Amber, Rhyme, Balmy, Limit, Empty. Bonus: Marble

162

46. CryptoList: Broadway Musicals

My Fair Lady, The Phantom of the Opera, Cats, Oklahoma, Grease, A Chorus Line, Miss Saigon, Evita, South Pacific, West Side Story

47. Letter by Letter Challenger

48. You Still Can't Miss!

A. End, B. Par

49. Splits on Ice!

Frosty, Arctic, Flurry, Freeze, Chilly, Flakes, Shovel, Winter, Icicle, Drifts, Anorak, Powder

50. Jumble Jacks

5 Letters: snare, raise, gripe, spare, organ
6 Letters: sniper, spring, senior
7 Letters: regions, persona, reaping, ignores
8 Letters: spongier
9 Letters: Singapore

51. A Heroic Mess

Answer: Arnold Schwarzenegger

52. Confusing Creatures

A. spigot, B. coward, C. knowledge, D. hyphen, E. location,
F. chapel, G. dogma

53. Build-a-Word Bonanza

Cheap metal	T	I	N							
Hue	T	I	N	T						
Bad smell	S	T	I	N	K					
Eye part	R	E	T	I	N	A				
A cocktail	M	A	R	T	I	N	I			
Meant to be	D	E	S	T	I	N	E	D		
Disturbing	U	P	S	E	T	T	I	N	G	
Examine closely	S	C	R	U	T	I	N	I	Z	E
Rude	I	M	P	E	R	T	I	N	E	N	T

54. A Crafty Clue Search

A. 4 gemstones: diamond, pearl, topaz, emerald

B. 5th American president: Monroe

C. A palindrome you can paddle: kayak

D. 3 colors beginning with the letter P: purple, plum,
   periwinkle

E. 3 types of windstorms: cyclone, typhoon, hurricane

55. The Luckiest Letters

Hamburger: 1. short, 2. acorn, 3. whims, 4. probe, 5. unite,
6. color, 7. bring, 8. guest, 9. blurt

56. A Wild-er Quotation

The only thing worse than being talked about is not being talked
about.

57. Lose-a-Letter Challenger

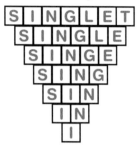

58. Do you miss me?

A. Fur, B. Bun

59. Calling All Letters

Other answers may be possible.

QuicK, EXempT, ZebrA, FresH, JokeR, VenoM, UNfolD, BrinG, WorrY, PicnIC, LOwerS

60. Vowel Play

There are several answers. "Facetious" is one.

61. Build-a-Word Brain Buster

A single unit	O	N	E							
Finished	D	O	N	E						
Cash	M	O	N	E	Y					
Earlier	S	O	O	N	E	R				
Burdensome	O	N	E	R	O	U	S			
First settlers	P	I	O	N	E	E	R	S		
Element	C	O	M	P	O	N	E	N	T	
Italian cheese	M	A	S	C	A	R	P	O	N	E
Church member	P	A	R	I	S	H	I	O	N	E	R

62. Jumpin' Jumbles!

5 Letters: speed, steep, spend, spied, preen, strip
6 Letters: spider, pester, esprit, priest, sprite
7 Letters: stipend, despite, striped, serpent
8 Letters: sprinted, pretends
9 Letters: president

63. A Devious Diamond

Him, Cream, Typical, Onion, Sea

64. SplitSplat!

Omelet, Waffle, Quiche, Cereal, Blintz, Crepes, Muffin, Coffee, Banana, Yogurt, Pastry, Muesli

65. Box Cross with a Twist

There are several possible solutions.

B	A	S	S
A	R	E	A
S	E	A	L
S	A	L	T

66. A Periodic Puzzler

Mercury, Zinc, Carbon, Iron, Oxygen, Arsenic, Copper, Silver, Nitrogen, Sodium

67. Shuffle, Hop, Step

Mikhail Baryshnikov

68. The Kitchen Sink

A. Pan, B. Pot, C. Cup, D. Dish

69. Clue Search Master Edition

A. 4 states beginning with the letter M: Mississippi, Maine, Michigan, Montana

B. 3 five-letter words beginning with the letter Q: Quote, Quake, Quest

C. 1988 Oscar-winning film: *Rain Man*

D. 3 Army ranks: Captain, Major, General

E. 3 racquet sports: Tennis, Badminton, Squash

70. CryptoList: Car Makers

Rolls-Royce, Lamborghini, Porsche, Lexus, Ferrari, Land Rover, Mitsubishi, Volkswagen, Toyota, Mercedes-Benz

71. More Switcheroo!

Theme = Clock: Hand, Face, Time, Hour, Tick

72. A Puzzle as Easy as A, B, C?

Answer: There are several answers. "Absconded" is one.

73. G Whiz!

Nudge, Sugar, Image, Egret, Urged, Bonus: GENIUS

74. Box Cross with a Twist—Again!

There are several solutions. Here is one:

P	A	W	N
A	L	O	E
W	O	O	S
N	E	S	T

75. Double Take!

a. Philadelphia, b. industrious, c. whether, d. saturate, e. consonant, f. memento, g. infinite, h. tortoise

76. Switcheroo Fun!

Theme = Bread: Rye, Wheat, White, Grain, Corn

77. The Wild-est Quotation

Experience is the name every one gives to their mistakes.

78. Swing and Miss?

A. Dig, B. Prop

79. Doublets: Master Class

Other solutions are possible.

A. WHEAT, CHEAT, CHEAP, CHEEP, CREEP, CREED, BREED, BREAD

B. BREAD, BREAK, BLEAK, BLEAT, BLEST, BLAST, BOAST, TOAST

80. Jumblicious!

5 Letters: aorta, acorn, tonic, Cairo, actor, ratio

6 Letters: carton, cantor, cannot, nation

7 Letters: contain, Croatia

8 Letters: raincoat

9 Letters: carnation

81. More Matchmaking!

A. Penny, B. Hang, C. Check, D. Skate

MathPlay Answer Section

1. A Baaaa Bender

9 sheep and 18 turkeys.

2. An Even Exchange

10, 12, 14, 16

3. Starter Sequence

A. 5, 10: Odd-numbered terms are increasing by one: 3, 4, 5 . . .
   and even-numbered terms are also increasing by one: 7, 8, 9 . . .

B. 11, 13: Odd-numbered terms are increasing by three: 1, 4, 7 . . .
   and even-numbered terms are also increasing by three: 2, 5, 8 . . .

C. 4, 1: Odd-numbered terms are decreasing by two: 7, 5, 3 . . . and
   even-numbered terms are also decreasing by two: 8, 6, 4 . . .

4. A Checkered Puzzle

5. Tell the Number

Answer: 16

6. A Starter Square

4	15	14	1
9	6	7	12
5	10	11	8
16	3	2	13

7. A Barnyard Brainteaser

180 spiders, 150 goats, and 30 ducks

8. A Cyclical Dilemma

Two full turns

9. An Age-Old Question

Jodi is 40; Hannah is 10.

10. Triangular Magic

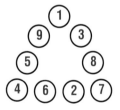

11. A Birthday Baffler

Jane is 12. Uncle John is 48.

12. A Not So Sneaky Square

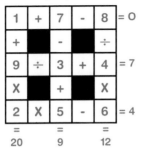

1	+	7	-	8	= 0
+	■	-	■	÷	
9	÷	3	+	4	= 7
X	■	+	■	X	
2	X	5	-	6	= 4
=		=		=	
20		9		12	

13. A Plethora of Nines
99 + 99/99

14. A Simple Split?
Use Roman numerals. When XI is split horizontally, VI is left on top.

15. A Deck of Trouble
Take the bottom row of 2 3 A and make it the top row. The square
will then be:

$$2\ 3\ A$$
$$A\ 2\ 3$$
$$3\ A\ 2$$

You have moved only three cards.

16. A Cubic Matter
A three-inch cube painted on the surface and divided into one-inch
cubes would form twenty-seven small cubes, of which eight would
have paint on three sides; twelve would have paint on two sides
only; six would have paint on one side only; and one would have no
paint at all.

17. A Series of Sequences

A. 4, 7: Odd-numbered terms (every other number) are increasing by one: 2, 3, 4 . . . and even-numbered terms are decreasing by one: 9, 8, 7 . . .

B. 8, 32: Odd-numbered terms (every other number) are doubling: 1, 2, 4, 8 . . . and even-numbered terms are doubling: 4, 8, 16

C. 21, 34: Each term equals the sum of the two previous terms.

18. A Digital Arrangement

$1 + 2 + 3 + 4 + 5 + 6 + 7 + (8 \times 9)$

19. Tommy's Toy Run

3 video games, 41 packs of baseball cards, and 56 plastic dinosaurs

20. Magic Square

21. Another Problem of Age

My son is 9.

22. Lock Box

100. Logic: In each box, the numbers in the right hand column are the squares of the numbers in the left hand column.

23. Applesauce

John took 16 apples.

24. Simple Subtraction?

From XIX, take I and leave XX

25. Hog Central

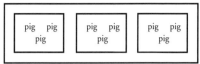

26. Warning! An Addition Problem

Be on guard. B = 1, E = 2, O = 3, N = 4, G = 5, U = 6, A = 7, R = 8, and D = 9. 1 + 32 + 64 + 59 + 78 = 234

27. Coin Sorter

A half dollar, a quarter, and four dimes

28. A Beach Build

204 times. The base layer is 8 x 8 which requires 64 cylinders. The next layer is 7 x 7 which requires 49 cylinders, and so on. 64 + 49 + 36 + 25 + 16 + 9 + 4 + 1 = 204.

29. A Moving Problem

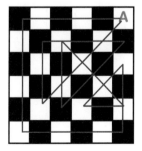

30. Tommy's Tangle

One half dollar, 39 dimes, and 60 pennies.

31. A Little More Triangular Magic

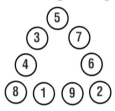

32. Mixed-Up Dominoes

2	1	3	3	3	2
2	2	1	1	2	3
3	4	1	2	1	5
5	3	4	5	1	4

33. Another Sneaky Square

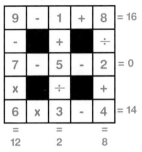

34. The Confused Commuter

18 miles

35. The Square Doughnut

Here is one solution:

11	1	7	8
4			12
3			5
9	10	6	2

36. Another Lock Box

26. Logic: In each box, the product of the top two numbers equals the product of the bottom two numbers.

37. Some Serious Sequences

A. S, O: Each letter is the first letter of the month beginning with J for January.

B. 21, 28: The first term equals 1, the second term is the sum of 1 + 2, the third term is the sum of 1 + 2 + 3, the fourth term is the sum of 1 + 2 + 3 + 4 . . .

C. 38, 39: The pattern is Add 1, Multiply by 2. Odd-numbered terms are twice the previous term. Even-numbered terms are one more than the previous term.

38. Criss Cross

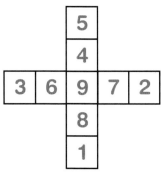

39. A Fishy Question

The head is 3 inches long. The tail is 3 inches long. The body is 9 inches long.

40. Puzzling in Peoria

74 miles

A 16-acre square field, with a fence around it, when divided into one-acre lots, would have four subdivisions fenced on two sides; eight subdivisions fenced on one side only; and four subdivisions with no fenced side.

2	4	4	5	5
4	2	3	4	5
4	1	1	3	3
3	2	1	3	5
1	1	5	3	2
2	5	1	4	2

9. Logic: In each box, the sum of all four numbers equals 49.

40 inches

15 + 36 + 47 + 2 = 100

46. Making More Magic!

17	24	1	8	15
23	5	7	14	16
4	6	13	20	22
10	12	19	21	3
11	18	25	2	9

47. The Missing Number

43. Each number's digits add up to 7.

48. The Lady and the Eggs

301 eggs

49. A Head Full of Numbers

11. Look carefully and you will notice that all of the numbers cancel themselves out.

50. A Puzzling Playgroup

13 friends and 64 marbles

51. Triple Play

The digit is 2: 2 + 22 = 24

52. A Super Sneaky Square

1	+	9	x	2	= 20

The grid:

1	+	9	x	2	= 20
x		÷		x	
6	x	3	-	5	= 13
+		x		+	
7	x	8	÷	4	= 14
= 13		= 24		= 14	

53. A Money Issue

S + M must equal a two-digit number, therefore M is 1. Since M is 1, S must be 9 (or else their sum would not be a two-digit number). S + M therefore equals 10, therefore O must equal 0. N + R must also equal a two-digit number, where the 1 is carried to the next column since E + 0 alone cannot equal N. Therefore N is a digit one more than E. The remaining possible combinations for N and E are 8 and 7, 7 and 6, 6 and 5, 5 and 4, 4 and 3, and 3 and 2. By trial and error, it quickly becomes apparent that the only combination that will result in a correct addition problem is where N = 6 and R = 8:

$$
\begin{array}{r}
9\,5\,6\,7 \\
+\ 1\,0\,8\,5 \\
\hline
1\,0\,6\,5\,2
\end{array}
$$

54. A Dastardly Criss Cross

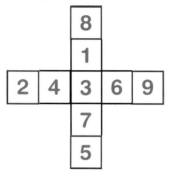

55. The Growing Tree

4 feet. Trees grow from the top, not from the base.

56. A Tricky Lock Box

5. Logic: In each box, the sum of the diagonals is equal.

57. Sequences: Master Class

A. 18: Multiply the two digits of the previous term together then subtract that result from the original number, i.e. 84 – (8 x 4) = 52; 52 – (5 x 2) = 42; . . . 22 – (2 x 2) = 18

B. 504: The first term is the product of 1 x 2 x 3 = 6, the second term is the product of 2 x 3 x 4 = 24, the third term is the product of 3 x 4 x 5 = 60 . . .

C. 312211: This is a descriptive sequence. The first term is 1, so we can say we have one "1", and so the second term is 11. Now we can say that we have two "1"s, and so the third term is 21. Since 21 has one "2" and one "1", the fourth term is 1211. Then, 1211 has one "1", one "2", and two "1"s and so the fifth term is 111221. 111221 can be described as three "1"s, two "2"s and one "1" and so the missing term is 312211.

58. A Puzzle of Pies

2 pies. At each town, Penny must give half of her pies, but she receives one back. If she has two pies, she gives each tax collector one pie which is then returned.

59. A Trickier Challenge

1 3 4 5 2 (13 x 4 = 52)

60. Too Much Wine?

1. Fill the 5-gallon cask. 2. Fill the 3-gallon cask with wine out of the 5-gallon cask; and empty those three gallons back into the 8-gallon cask. 3. Now that the 3-gallon cask is empty, fill it with the remaining two gallons from the 5-gallon cask. 5. Once again, fill the 5-gallon cask from the wine in the 8-gallon cask. Only 1 gallon will now remain in the 8-gallon cask. 6. Then from the 5-gallon cask, fill the 3-gallon cask—which requires only 1 gallon to top it off, thereby leaving four gallons in the 5-gallon cask. 7. Empty the 3-gallon cask into the 8-gallon cask, and now you will have four gallons there.

61. Serious about Cereal

20 boxes. From the original 81 box tops, Robin will get 16 boxes of cereal and still have 1 box top remaining. With those 17 box tops (from the 16 boxes of cereal and her 1 spare), Robin will receive 3 more boxes of cereal with 2 box tops remaining. With those 5 box tops (from the 3 boxes of cereal and the 2 spare), she will receive one last box of cereal.

62. The Sneakiest Square

4	÷	2	x	8	= 16
-	■	+	■	÷	
3	x	7	-	4	= 17
+	■	-	■	+	
9	x	1	-	6	= 3
=		=		=	
10		8		8	

63. A Dastardly Doughnut

5	11	4	6
12			9
2			3
7	10	1	8

64. Cracking the Combination

1 2 4 8 16

65. A Poker Puzzle

As 24 different sequences are possible, the banquets are held 25 weeks apart (the poker game being skipped on the evening of the banquet). If the position of a sequence with reference to the chairs were counted, the total arrangements would be 5 x 4 x 3 x 2 x 1 (=120). But the position of a sequence with reference to the chairs is not counted by the Club. As any given sequence may sit in five positions with reference to the chairs, the 120 must be divided by 5. Thus the answer is 24.

66. Not-So-Simple Division

From the last subtraction, G is seen to be 0. The second subtraction gives K as 1. The first subtraction shows that T is one greater than H, and the last shows that B is one greater than T. Hence, H T B are in ascending sequence; the second subtraction shows that H plus B equals 10; these three letters then must stand for 4, 5, and 6. You can then easily determine the following: U=2, D=3, M=7, E=8, and R=9.

```
              2 2 7
    4 3 7 ) 9 9 5 0 6
            8 7 4
            ─────
            1 2 1 0
              8 7 4
              ─────
              3 3 6 6
              3 0 5 9
              ───────
                3 0 7
```

1:12 pm. If x is the number of hours that have elapsed since noon, then $(6 - x)$ is the number of hours until 6 PM, then:

$x = \frac{1}{3} + \frac{1}{6}(6-x)$

$x = \frac{1}{3}x + 1 - \frac{1}{6}x$

$x = \frac{1}{6}x + 1$

$\frac{5}{6}x = 1$

$x = \frac{6}{5}$ hours

Since $1\frac{1}{5}$ hours equals 1 hour and 12 minutes, the time is 1:12 PM.

LogicPlay Answer Section

1. Tricky Train Travel

1 hour and 10 minutes is equal to 70 minutes.

2. Riddle for the Ages

That man is my son. I am his father.

3. A Calculating Conundrum

Four. If a fourth of forty were six, a half of forty would be twelve and a third of twenty (now twelve) would be four.

4. A River Runs Through It

Take the goose over. Return and take the fox over and bring the goose back. Leave the goose on the bank, and take the corn over. Then return for the goose.

5. Udderly Puzzling?

Three

6. All in a Day's Work

Since Charlene is taller than the editor, she is not the editor nor can she be the chef, who is the shortest. Charlene is therefore the banker.

	ALICE	BETTY	CHARLENE
BANKER	X	X	YES
EDITOR			X
CHEF			X

Since Alice has a brother, she is therefore not an only child and cannot be the chef. Therefore she is the editor.

	ALICE	BETTY	CHARLENE
BANKER	X	X	YES
EDITOR	YES		X
CHEF	X		X

By process of elimination then, Betty is the chef.

	ALICE	BETTY	CHARLENE
BANKER	X	X	YES
EDITOR	YES	X	X
CHEF	X	YES	X

7. Disorganized Dishes!

Since the color is not specified, you need only choose three dishes from the cabinet to ensure a matching pair.

8. Montezuma's Muddle

The big Aztec was his mother.

9. The Puzzling Penthouse

The man is extremely short. He can easily reach the ground floor elevator button, but he cannot reach the elevator button for the penthouse as it is too high. He can only reach halfway up the elevator buttons, forcing him to walk the remaining flights. However, if it is raining, then he will have his umbrella with him and can press the higher buttons using it.

10. Double Trouble

The girls are two of a set of triplets (or quadruplets, etc.).

11. A Family Matter

Since John is older than Larry, he is not the youngest; and, according to the last statement, John does not have red hair. Therefore John has brown hair.

	SUZANNE	JOHN	LARRY
HAIR COLOR		BROWN	
AGE			

Since Larry does not have blond hair, he therefore must have red hair and Suzanne must be the blond.

	SUZANNE	JOHN	LARRY
HAIR COLOR	BLOND	BROWN	RED
AGE			

Since the youngest child is blond, Suzanne must be 11. Since John is older than Larry, John must be 15 and Larry must therefore be 14.

	SUZANNE	JOHN	LARRY
HAIR COLOR	BLOND	BROWN	RED
AGE	11	15	14

12. It's in the Bag!

There were only three people shopping: a grandmother, a mother, and a daughter. The "mother" is counted as both a mother and a daughter.

13. A Dirty Dilemma

None

14. Think Before You Leap

38 days. He jumps all the way out the last day.

15. The Cider Barrel

Jimmy and the farmer tipped the barrel until the cider was just about to overflow. (The top was evidently off, since Jimmy "looked into the barrel.") If any of the bottom were visible, it would mean that the barrel was less than half full; while if none of the bottom were visible, it would mean that the barrel was at least half full.

16. My Three Sons

Since Alex or Ben is the shortest, then Craig must NOT be the shortest.

	ALEX	BEN	CRAIG
TALLEST			
MIDDLE			
SHORTEST			X

Since Craig is indeed not the shortest, then Alex is the tallest.

	ALEX	BEN	CRAIG
TALLEST	YES	X	X
MIDDLE	X		
SHORTEST	X		X

By process of elimination then, Craig must be of middle height.

	ALEX	BEN	CRAIG
TALLEST	YES	X	X
MIDDLE	X	X	YES
SHORTEST	X		X

Also by process of elimination, Ben must therefore be the shortest.

	ALEX	BEN	CRAIG
TALLEST	YES	X	X
MIDDLE	X	X	YES
SHORTEST	X	YES	X

17. On Board!

The trains would be the same distance from New York when they meet.

18. A Space Odyssey

Two. The chief takes two astronauts with him. For the first hour's leg, Astronaut #1 gives oxygen to himself, the chief, and Astronaut #2, and then uses his last hour of oxygen to return back to the station. For the second hour's leg, Astronaut #2 gives oxygen to himself and to the chief, and then uses his remaining two hours of oxygen to return back to the station. The chief now uses his own four hours of oxygen to travel the final four legs to the Russian station.

19. A Marital Mystery

The husband is a photographer. He took a picture of his wife and then developed it.

20. The Mixed-up Florist

First, assume statement 1 is true, and his sister received roses, his wife received carnations, and therefore his mother received lilies. However, statement 3 contradicts this. Therefore his sister could not have received roses.

	WIFE	SISTER	MOTHER
ROSES		X	
CARNATIONS			
LILIES			

Because the sister did not receive roses, we know therefore from statement 2 that his mother did not receive carnations.

	WIFE	SISTER	MOTHER
ROSES		X	
CARNATIONS			X
LILIES			

Since his mother did not receive carnations, statement 5 cannot be true, and his wife therefore could not receive roses.

	WIFE	SISTER	MOTHER
ROSES	X	X	
CARNATIONS			X
LILIES			

By process of elimination, then, his mother received the roses.

	WIFE	SISTER	MOTHER
ROSES	X	X	YES
CARNATIONS			X
LILIES			X

According to statement 4, if his mother received the roses, then his wife received the lilies. By process of elimination then, his sister received the carnations.

	WIFE	SISTER	MOTHER
ROSES	X	X	YES
CARNATIONS	X	YES	X
LILIES	YES	X	X

21. The Man of the Family

The easiest way to solve this puzzle is to set up the family tree:

A. 27 pairs of cousins
B. 12 pairs of father and son
C. 12 pairs of brothers
D. 18 pairs of uncle and nephew
E. 9 pairs of grandfather and grandson

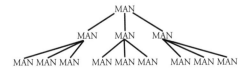

22. A Leap of Logic

The man was a window washer. He slid open the window and jumped inside.

23. Another Leap of Logic

The plane is on the ground.

24. A Dinner Cruise?

Cannibal YumYum takes one cannibal over and leaves him. He then takes another cannibal and leaves him. When Cannibal YumYum returns with the boat, two anthropologists go over, one of them remaining while the other returns, bringing a cannibal with him. One anthropologist then goes over with Cannibal YumYum. An anthropologist returns with a cannibal, but leaves Cannibal YumYum on the other side. The two anthropologists then cross over and turn over the boat to Cannibal YumYum, who makes two other trips for the cannibals, bringing one at a time.

25. Code Cracker

26. Frank, Connor, and Slick

I. cannot be Frank because he would be telling a lie, nor can he be Connor because he would be telling the truth. Therefore B is Slick. C therefore must be Frank as he telling the truth, and so A must be Connor.

II. B must be Frank because C certainly can't be Frank, and if A were Frank, there is no false statement left for Connor to claim. Connor is therefore A, as that is the only remaining statement that he could claim falsely. C then is Slick.

III. is not Frank because he would then be lying. B is not Frank because then A would have to be Connor, and he would be telling the truth. Therefore, C is Frank, B is Connor, and A is Slick.

IV. B cannot be Connor because he would be telling the truth, nor can B be Frank as he would be telling a lie. Therefore B is Slick. A is therefore telling the truth and must be Frank and C must be Connor.

V. A cannot be Frank as then all three statements are true and there is no statement that Connor could have made. A cannot be Connor as he would be telling the truth. Therefore A is Slick. B must be Connor for it is the only statement he can make falsely. And so C is Frank.

VI. A cannot be Frank as that would mean B is Connor and C is Slick, and Connor would now be making a true statement. B also cannot be Frank as that would mean C is Slick and A is Connor, and again Connor would be making a true statement. C therefore must be Frank, and so B is Slick and A is Connor.

VII. C cannot be Frank as he would be telling a lie. If A is Frank, then B must be Connor and C must be Slick, but this is impossible as Connor would be telling the truth. Therefore, Frank must be B and telling the truth that C is Slick. A then is Connor.

VIII. B can't be Slick because then Frank and Connor would be accusing him of being Slick, and Connor cannot tell the truth. And if B isn't Slick, then neither A nor C can be Frank, since they wouldn't be telling the truth. Therefore, B is Frank. It then follows that C is Slick and A is Connor.

27. A Clubby Affair

Based on statement 1, neither Jim nor Joe is the dentist. Based on statement 2, Jack is not the lawyer. Based on statement 3, Joe is not the doctor. Based on statement 4, Jerry is neither the banker nor the lawyer.

	JIM	JACK	JOE	JERRY
BANKER				X
DENTIST	X		X	
DOCTOR			X	
LAWYER		X		X

Joe must either be the banker or the lawyer. However, the banker cannot be Joe, because according to statement 4, the banker is friendly with two of the three other men, while according to statement 1, Joe is unfriendly with two of the other three men. Therefore, Joe is the lawyer.

	JIM	JACK	JOE	JERRY
BANKER			X	X
DENTIST	X		X	
DOCTOR			X	
LAWYER	X	X	YES	X

According to statement 2, Jack and Joe (the lawyer) are friends, but statement 1 indicates that Jack is not friendly with the dentist. Therefore Jack cannot be the dentist. By process of elimination, then, Jerry is the dentist.

	JIM	JACK	JOE	JERRY
BANKER			X	X
DENTIST	X	X	X	YES
DOCTOR			X	X
LAWYER	X	X	YES	X

According to statement 4, the banker is friendly with Joe (the lawyer) while according to statement 1, Jim and Joe are unfriendly. So the banker cannot be Jim, and so by process of elimination must be Jack. Therefore, also by process of elimination, the doctor must be Jim.

	JIM	JACK	JOE	JERRY
BANKER	X	YES	X	X
DENTIST	X	X	X	YES
DOCTOR	YES	X	X	X
LAWYER	X	X	YES	X

28. A Revolutionary Problem

As proof that Robespierre did not execute his personal enemies as enemies of the state, was the simple fact that his personal enemies were still living to bring the charges against him. Anyone who thus accused him automatically disproved the charge. If Robespierre had followed the practice of which he was accused, there would have been no one present to attack him.

29. Sibling Logic

The nephew of the man was the son of the man's sister.

30. A Picnic Poser

The poison in the lemonade came from the ice cubes. When Samantha drank the lemonade, the ice cubes were fully frozen. As time elapsed, the ice melted and the poison mixed into the lemonade.

31. A Cook's Conundrum

Statements (2) and (3) may both be true, but cannot both be false. Statements (1) and (3) may both be false, but cannot both be true.

32. The Housing Crisis

For each position (1st, 2nd, 3rd, etc.), there is a neighbor, a painter, and a color associated with it. From statement B, we know that "Charlie" and "Brown" are a unit. Likewise, from statement C, we know that "Mrs. Roberts" and "Yellow" are a unit, and from statement D, we know that "Mr. Smith" and "Paul" are a unit.

From statements F, G, and H, we know the following:

	1ST	2ND	3RD	4TH	5TH
NEIGHBOR			MILLER		
PAINTER				MATT	
COLOR					GREEN

Statement H also tells us that neither Charlie nor Henry painted the third house. We already know that Matt did not paint it, and since Paul paints Mr. Smith's house (statement D), then Aaron must paint Mr. Miller's house.

	1ST	2ND	3RD	4TH	5TH
NEIGHBOR			MILLER		
PAINTER			AARON	MATT	
COLOR					GREEN

From statements B and E, we know that Charlie did not paint the second house brown. Therefore Charlie must have painted the first house brown, as "Charlie" and "Brown" are a unit, and there is no other possible placement.

	1ST	2ND	3RD	4TH	5TH
NEIGHBOR			MILLER		
PAINTER	CHARLIE		AARON	MATT	
COLOR	BROWN				GREEN

From statement C, we know that "Mrs. Roberts" and "Yellow" are a unit, and Matt cannot be her painter. Then the second house must be Mrs. Roberts' yellow house.

	1ST	2ND	3RD	4TH	5TH
NEIGHBOR		ROBERTS	MILLER		
PAINTER	CHARLIE		AARON	MATT	
COLOR	BROWN	YELLOW			GREEN

From statement G, we know that Matt did not paint his client's house white, therefore the third house must be white and the fourth house must be red. Additionally, since "Mr. Smith" and "Paul" are a unit, they must be the neighbor and painter for the fifth house.

	1ST	2ND	3RD	4TH	5TH
NEIGHBOR		ROBERTS	MILLER		SMITH
PAINTER	CHARLIE		AARON	MATT	PAUL
COLOR	BROWN	YELLOW	WHITE	RED	GREEN

Finally, since statement A indicates that Mrs. Bennett does not live in the first house, she must live in the fourth house. By process of elimination, then, Mr. Jones lives in the first house, and the 2nd house is painted by Henry.

	1ST	2ND	3RD	4TH	5TH
NEIGHBOR	JONES	ROBERTS	MILLER	BENNETT	SMITH
PAINTER	CHARLIE	HENRY	AARON	MATT	PAUL
COLOR	BROWN	YELLOW	WHITE	RED	GREEN

33. A Family Dilemma

There were present two sisters and their brother, their father and mother, and two paternal grandparents.

34. Code Cracker Rematch

♦ ● ■ ♣

35. The Sultan's Choice

The brainy courtier said: "If my cap were white, either one of my rivals would have known that his own was black, for the remaining man's raised hand showed that he saw a black cap—and that could not be mine if mine were white. But I waited a few minutes and neither one of my rivals dropped his hand to show that he knew the color of his cap. That meant that my cap could not be white and consequently must be black."

36. The Courtiers Choose Again!

The courtier in back would only be able to deduce his color cap if the two men in front of him were both wearing the white caps. Therefore, either or both the middle courtier and the front courtier are wearing a black cap. The middle courtier now knowing that either he and/or the courtier in front of him is wearing a black cap, responds that he too does not know what color cap he is wearing. However, if the middle courtier had seen the front man wearing a white cap, he would have deduced that he must have been wearing a black cap. Therefore, the middle courtier saw a black cap on the first courtier's head. Having heard both statements, the first courtier concluded thus.

37. A Puzzle of a Panel

1st: Rich Riddle, 2nd: Leah Laptop, 3rd: Caren Caravan, 4th: Rob Runner, 5th: Michele Mosaic, 6th: Cindy City, 7th: Lori Literati, 8th: S. Squeeze

From statement (2) we know that Rich Riddle does not sit in the 8th seat and Leah Laptop does not sit in the 1st seat. From statement (3) we know that Michele Mosaic does not sit in the 1st seat nor can she sit in the 6th, 7th, or 8th seat. And since S. Squeeze sits three seats to the right of Michele Mosaic, S. Squeeze cannot sit in the 1st, 2nd, 3rd, or 4th seat. From statement (4) we know that Lori Literati cannot sit in the 1st, 2nd, 3rd, 4th, or 8th seat, and therefore Caren Caravan cannot sit in the 4th, 5th, 6th, 7th, or 8th seat.

	1ST	2ND	3RD	4TH	5TH	6TH	7TH	8TH
CAREN CARAVAN				X	X	X	X	X
CINDY CITY								
LEAH LAPTOP	X							
LORI LITERATI	X	X	X	X				X
MICHELE MOSAIC	X					X	X	X
ROB RUNNER								
RICH RIDDLE								X
S. SQUEEZE	X	X	X	X				

From statement (5) we know that the seating arrangement must contain the block:

| LEAH | | ROB | | CINDY |

Therefore, Rob Runner cannot sit in the 1st, 2nd, 7th, or 8th seat. Also, Leah Laptop cannot sit in the 7th or 8th seat and Cindy City cannot sit in the 1st or 2nd seat.

	1ST	2ND	3RD	4TH	5TH	6TH	7TH	8TH
CAREN CARAVAN				X	X	X	X	X
CINDY CITY	X	X						
LEAH LAPTOP	X						X	X
LORI LITERATI	X	X	X	X				X
MICHELE MOSAIC	X					X	X	X
ROB RUNNER	X	X					X	X
RICH RIDDLE								X
S. SQUEEZE	X	X	X	X				

Since we already know that Leah Laptop cannot sit in the first seat, Rob Runner therefore cannot sit in the 3rd seat (two seats to her right) and Cindy City cannot sit in the 5th seat (two seats to his right).

	1ST	2ND	3RD	4TH	5TH	6TH	7TH	8TH
CAREN CARAVAN				X	X	X	X	X
CINDY CITY	X	X			X			
LEAH LAPTOP	X						X	X
LORI LITERATI	X	X	X	X				X
MICHELE MOSAIC	X					X	X	X
ROB RUNNER	X	X	X				X	X
RICH RIDDLE								X
S. SQUEEZE	X	X	X	X				

Since the first seat now open to Rob Runner is the 4th seat, then Cindy City cannot sit any farther left than the 6th seat. Therefore, Cindy City does not sit in the 1st through 5th seats. And since the 6th seat is the farthest right seat in which Rob Runner can sit, Leah Laptop cannot sit in the 5th or 6th seat.

	1ST	2ND	3RD	4TH	5TH	6TH	7TH	8TH
CAREN CARAVAN				X	X	X	X	X
CINDY CITY	X	X	X	X	X			
LEAH LAPTOP					X	X	X	X
LORI LITERATI	X	X	X	X				X
MICHELE MOSAIC	X					X	X	X
ROB RUNNER	X	X	X				X	X
RICH RIDDLE								X
S. SQUEEZE	X	X	X	X				

We can also determine that Leah Laptop cannot sit in the 3rd or 4th seat. If she did, there would be no seat available for Lori Literati—since from statement (1), we know that Lori Literati can't sit next to Leah Laptop and from statement (4), we know that Lori Literati can't sit between Rob Runner and Cindy City. If Leah Laptop cannot sit in the 3rd or 4th seat, then it follows that Rob Runner cannot sit in the 5th or 6th seat, nor can Cindy City sit in the 7th or 8th seat.

	1ST	2ND	3RD	4TH	5TH	6TH	7TH	8TH
CAREN CARAVAN				X	X	X	X	X
CINDY CITY	X	X	X	X	X		X	X
LEAH LAPTOP			X	X	X	X	X	X
LORI LITERATI	X	X	X	X				X
MICHELE MOSAIC	X					X	X	X
ROB RUNNER	X	X			X	X	X	X
RICH RIDDLE								X
S. SQUEEZE	X	X	X	X				

Dr. S. Squeeze must sit in the 8th seat as no one else can. From statement (3), we therefore can determine that Michele Mosaic must sit in the 5th seat.

	1ST	2ND	3RD	4TH	5TH	6TH	7TH	8TH
CAREN CARAVAN				X	X	X	X	X
CINDY CITY	X	X	X	X	X		X	X
LEAH LAPTOP			X	X	X	X	X	X
LORI LITERATI	X	X	X	X				X
MICHELE MOSAIC	X	X	X	X	YES	X	X	X
ROB RUNNER	X	X			X	X	X	X
RICH RIDDLE					X			X
S. SQUEEZE	X	X	X	X	X	X	X	YES

Cindy City must sit in the 6th seat as there is no other seat available for her. Thus, Rob Runner sits in the 4th seat and Leah Laptop sits in the 2nd seat.

	1ST	2ND	3RD	4TH	5TH	6TH	7TH	8TH
CAREN CARAVAN		X		X	X	X	X	X
CINDY CITY	X	X	X	X	X	YES	X	X
LEAH LAPTOP	X	YES	X	X	X	X	X	X
LORI LITERATI	X	X	X	X	X	X		X
MICHELE MOSAIC	X	X	X	X	YES	X	X	X
ROB RUNNER	X	X	X	YES	X	X	X	X
RICH RIDDLE		X		X	X	X		
S. SQUEEZE	X	X	X	X	X	X	X	YES

Lori Literati must sit in the 7th seat, the only available seat remaining to her. Thus Caren Caravan must sit in the 3rd seat, and Rich Riddle must sit in the 1st seat.

	1ST	2ND	3RD	4TH	5TH	6TH	7TH	8TH
CAREN CARAVAN	X	X	YES	X	X	X	X	X
CINDY CITY	X	X	X	X	X	YES	X	X
LEAH LAPTOP	X	YES	X	X	X	X	X	X
LORI LITERATI	X	X	X	X	X	X	YES	X
MICHELE MOSAIC	X	X	X	X	YES	X	X	X
ROB RUNNER	X	X	X	YES	X	X	X	X
RICH RIDDLE	YES	X	X	X	X	X	X	X
S. SQUEEZE	X	X	X	X	X	X	X	YES